Dedication • Inspiration • Empathy • Faith • Giving • Trust
Commitment • Soulmate • Enthusiasm • Supportive • Thoug
Communication • Patience • Compassion • Dedication • Inspiration
Romance • Sharing • Desire • Humor • Commitment • Soulmate • Enthusiasm • Supporti
Hugs & Kisses • Fun • Harmony • Communication • Patience • Compassion • Dedication
Laughter • Hope • Passion • Contentment • Romance • Sharing • Desire • Humor • Commitmen
Understanding • Joy • Devotion • Caring • Hugs & Kisses • Fun • Harmony • Communication
Kindness • Companionship • Laughter • Hope • Passion • Contentment • Romance • Sharing
Forgiving • Togetherness • Love • Understanding • Joy • Devotion • Caring • Hugs & Kisses • Fun
Giving • Trust • Honesty • Bliss • Kindness • Companionship • Laughter • Hope • Passion
Thoughtful • Happiness • Forgiving • Togetherness • Love • Understanding • Joy • Devotion
Inspiration • Empathy • Faith • Giving • Trust • Honesty • Bliss • Kindness • Companionship
Soulmate • Enthusiasm • Supportive • Thoughtful • Happiness • Forgiving • Togetherness • Lov
Patience • Compassion • Dedication • Inspiration • Empathy • Faith • Giving • Trust • Honesty
Desire • Humor • Commitment • Soulmate • Enthusiasm • Supportive • Thoughtful • Happines
Harmony • Communication • Patience • Compassion • Dedication • Inspiration • Empathy • Fait
Romance • Sharing • Desire • Humor • Commitment • Soulmate • Enthusiasm • Supporti
Hugs & Kisses • Fun • Harmony • Communication • Patience • Compassion • Dedication
Laughter • Hope • Passion • Contentment • Romance • Sharing • Desire • Humor • Commitmen
Understanding • Joy • Devotion • Caring • Hugs & Kisses • Fun • Harmony • Communication
Kindness • Companionship • Laughter • Hope • Passion • Contentment • Romance • Sharing
Forgiving • Togetherness • Love • Understanding • Joy • Devotion • Caring • Hugs & Kisses • Fun

Everlasting Matrimony

PEARLS OF WISDOM FROM COUPLES MARRIED 50 YEARS OR MORE

BY SHERYL P. KURLAND

BAI
PUBLISHING

Library of Congress
Cataloging-in-Publication Data
ISBN 978-0-615-13997-5

Library of Congress Card Catalog Number:
2003097052

10 9 8 7 6 5 4 3

Book and Jacket Design:
Laura H. Couallier, Laura Herrmann Design

Published by

BAI
PUBLISHING

P.O. Box 917172
Longwood, Florida 32779
TEL 407-786-7747

Manufactured in China

*Dedicated to
the 75 couples who
participated in this book*

Introduction

No one knows more about the ingredients embodying a long-lasting, rich and loving marriage than couples married 50 years or longer. *Everlasting Matrimony: Pearls Of Wisdom From Couples Married 50 Years Or More* is a collection of words of wisdom and advice from husbands and wives who, at minimum, have celebrated their golden anniversaries. The couples reside across the United States and in Canada, and represent different faiths, cultures and ethnicities. Their candid insight touches upon every aspect of marriage — ranging from communication, sex and money to children, religion, hardships and much more.

Why did I write *Everlasting Matrimony*? To fill a void: Getting straight talk from the *experts*.

Specifically, research and revelation led up to the idea for developing this book. Here's what I learned: 1) Studies indicate that the divorce rate in the United States is one of the highest in the world. Fifty-percent of first marriages end in divorce. The likelihood of divorce in second or higher-order marriages is even greater; 2) Libraries and bookstores are saturated with self-help psychology books analyzing the dynamics of relationships, but readers tend to find them complex or too boring to finish; 3) The media glamorizes celebrity split-ups, giving them headline attention and making it seem like divorcing a spouse is as ordinary as spilling out a bad cup of coffee; 4) Couples considering marriage or who are currently married are demoralized, feeling they are doomed to eventual failure.

Where are *role models*? In *Everlasting Matrimony*.

Locating role model couples entailed running newspaper ads, contacting retirement communities, churches and synagogues, networking with friends and relatives, talking to strangers in restaurants, and using any other unique channels I could find. After the couples were located, each husband and wife responded separately to a series of questions: To what do you attribute your long-lasting marriage?; What advice would you give couples about to be married?; What do you wish you had known before entering matrimony? Their responses are contained herein. (Some couples preferred to answer jointly, expressing their unity and unbreakable bond.)

Naysayers might defensively reason that the featured couples have had successful marriages because "Times were a lot different back then." Indeed they were! These couples have lived through two world wars, a severe economic depression, and, minus the conveniences and technologies we take for granted today, daily life was much, much harder. Despite the challenges, the husbands and wives have possessed an untiring loyalty to their mate, and their drive to persevere *together* has never wavered.

Everlasting Matrimony is a treasure chest of lessons on marital bliss. Whether you're contemplating marriage, planning your wedding or you've been married 1, 5, 10, 25 years or beyond, you'll find there's always more to be learned.

David and Annette Alpert

MARRIED ON MAY 19, 1946
JACKSONVILLE, FLORIDA
HIS AGE: 22   HER AGE: 18

David knew Annette's sister-in-law, who discretely arranged for him to be at Annette's family's home when Annette was there. At the "event," her mother made David a scrumptious corned-beef sandwich which convinced him he wanted to be a member of Annette's family forever!

To achieve longevity within a marriage the following are most important, not necessarily in order of importance as they are listed:

1. **Commitment!** Total to your partner **and** to the relationship. The desire and determination that with work and positive attitudes…This union will succeed!

2. **Honesty, Fidelity, Integrity!** A sensitive attitude toward hearing your partner's words and thoughts, as well as in expressing your own. Enlarge upon your individual abilities to speak and listen. Work out any problems with a willingness to talk about them and a positive attitude toward solving them.

3. **Develop and practice a positive attitude toward change!** To remain healthy, a marriage must allow for growth, as individuals and as a couple.

4. **That which begins with a physical attraction needs time in which to grow and mature into love!** When we first met, there was a sexual attraction. (I also allow for the mental stimulation between the two parties.) However, I now realize that with time that original feeling becomes a very deep-seated bonding which I name **Love.** And I strongly repeat **Time** is needed for this development.

5. **Procreation = Children!** Whether the parties give birth to a child or children of their union or through an adoption process, I believe that rearing young ones and being part of that development process makes for a bonding, none of which can be surpassed. (CONTINUED ON PAGE 156)

Fortunately, we have been able to weather the storms and have enjoyed much, much happiness during our years together. There are many factors which have a bearing on whether a marriage can survive for many years, 50 or more. Some of the elements contributing to our long marriage are as follows:

1. This was a first marriage for both of us.

2. We were young when we tied the knot; my wife was 18 and I was 22.

3. We were both in fairly good health for our ages. Over our lives together we have had various health problems, some of which were serious. We have been able to work them out together.

4. In many ways we are different, but we do have strong common interests. Each of us has strengths as well as weaknesses. The object of life is to concentrate on our strengths and to bolster the weaknesses in our mate.

5. We have complete faith in each other as to integrity and fidelity. We have not allowed any situation to arise which would have created problems in this regard.

6. We have had differences over the years, some of which presented us with real problems. If our relationship together was not as strong as it is, our relationship would not have survived.

7. We are compatible with each other.

8. We have six children, who have provided us with grandchildren and great-grandchildren. (CONTINUED ON PAGE 156)

David

Edward and Iva Barnes

Married on September 7, 1930
Clarksfield, Ohio
His age: 21   Her age: 20

Iva and Edward became friendly during a number of joint classes at Columbia Union College. Edward had a girlfriend, but when the couple broke up he didn't waste a minute to hitch Iva.

arriage is a time to try right away to know what his goals are and try to keep them in mind. And it won't be long you are in harmony and know pretty well what his desires are. Try to blend your desires together. My husband and I had a great desire to follow the Lord too. We both love the out of doors and love studying different things in nature.

We were in college and that made things a bit different too. We both loved traveling. My husband earned all of his expenses so we both worked and cooperated.

I think one important thing is to show your appreciation of things that have been done for you, and thank your husband.

A lady said to me today, "You pat your husband on the arm or back just to let him know you love him and are mindful of his needs."

At first there seemed to be a few things but I tried to see what I could do to help the situation. Another thing we did was to have a stopping place and talk about our situation and see what we could do. That was helpful. Plan ahead. And loving the Lord has helped us a great deal.

More than 70 years have passed and we are **very** happy together and love each other.

Iva

he day we were married, Iva's cousin, Ira, took me aside and said "The Fairchild's get married for life. If you don't agree you should call the wedding off." We put our future in God's hands, and never turned back. We never let a disagreement fester overnight.

Our three children have brought much happiness. In our 70-plus years of marriage, we have had very strong support.

My wife is industrious, happy, and outgoing. Continually gives of herself. Loving and friendly.

Raymond and Winnifred Bartholomew

MARRIED ON NOVEMBER 28, 1942
BUFFALO, NEW YORK
HIS AGE: 18   HER AGE: 18

Lost & Found: Winnifred and her sister went to the movies as did Raymond and his buddy. The boys sat behind the girls and turned on their charm. Flirting continued afterward at an ice-cream parlor but when Raymond asked Winnifred for her phone number she refused to give it to him. Ironically, just weeks later, Winnifred's family moved next door to Raymond's sister. Raymond, at last, found his sweetheart.

The first thing I would tell a couple planning to marry is to find a person that they really love, one you would die for. Then put God first in your life and keep him close because you will be talking to him a lot. He is the only one that can solve the many problems that will pop up.

In all the years we have been married, we never fought over money. My husband always had two jobs and I worked part-time. The money went to paying bills and what was left was "ours." We never had our own bank accounts, always joint accounts. In our long life together we wanted the same things, what was important to Raymond was important to me. We were lucky to have parents that helped when they could. We went through a war, my husband got shot when hunting, and he lost his job which he had for 19 years (they went out of business).

When my husband got shot, the shock of that caused us to have a premature baby—3 lbs., 2 oz. She is now a beautiful woman in her fifties. Eleven months later we had a baby boy, which was a very difficult birth. It is the first time we saved both the mother and child. Ten years later we had a girl and three years later another boy. My youngest son was married two years when his beautiful wife died of cancer. Now he is married and has twins. We have nine wonderful grandchildren and four great-grandchildren.

My husband started having heart attacks at the age of 37. He has been sick most of his life with cluster headaches, diabetes, and heart problems.

I remember a time we couldn't afford a set of pillows so we shared one. It was fun and made us closer. (CONTINUED ON PAGE 156)

Winnifred

I believe a lasting marriage begins with taking the wedding vows seriously in front of God, and all witnesses: "Till death do us part" covers this life but because of the beautiful relationship we should hope that He would allow it to continue throughout eternity.

There are many definitions of the word "love"; but we must realize that our Heavenly Father created the word love.

All things created by Him that grow must be nourished by water and sunlight. For over 60 years, my beautiful wife has watered and furnished sunlight every day, allowing our marriage to flourish and grow.

Since going together, before and after marriage, we have had a saying: "If you love me, squeeze my hand, ouch, don't squeeze so hard, I know you love me." To this day we both still say "ouch"! The smile I get every morning seems to say "I forgive you for getting older and I love you more each day."

Personality and disposition can make for a great marriage or a disaster. My wife has never had a change in her personality or disposition in the years that I have known her. She's been the same loving and caring wife day in and day out. Our children can vouch for that. Because of their mother's concern for our marriage, our four children are on their way to successful marriages.

I worked for a company named General Baking or Bond bread. They had a package of donuts with printing that stated "Our doughnuts are gooder," but because of the bad English it was discontinued.

(CONTINUED ON PAGE 156)

Raymond

David and Jane Benjamin

Married on August 27, 1940
New York, New York
His age: 23   Her age: 18

David and Jane lived in the same apartment building at the same time in New York City but didn't get acquainted until a chance encounter at a party at Cornell University. They were with other dates, but struck up a conversation and discovered their similar home address. Thereafter, neighbors became locked in love.

*S*ome major ingredients would be **trusting**, **respecting**, **sharing**, **laughing** and **listening** to each other. For couples contemplating marriage, I would hope that their self-esteems were intact and that they were lucky enough not to have been too scarred, emotionally, in the process of growing up. Some of the positive arrangements in these 60-plus years of marriage include: similar backgrounds, worshipping together, an enormous appreciation of classical music which we can and do still enjoy, and sports of all kinds. We've also enjoyed skiing, sailing and tennis (which now, obviously have diminished), reading, our work, our play, friends, and individual pursuits. When I went back to college to get a degree that I did not get at the proper time, David was very supportive. David's tenderness and insistence that my sex life be as fulfilled as his was, and still is, a compensating factor in a lifetime filled with many trials and tribulations. On the down side, we both came from fatherless homes. My father died when I was three, his father died when he was six. Both men died tragic deaths. In that era, illness, dying and death were subjects not to be discussed with children. Parents were dishonest with us and I grew up knowing my Dad was **not** there, but his dying — how, why and when — were not mentioned. I wish we could have started our life together with **More Humor and Joy** in each day, with some of the wisdom we now have. I wish I had believed in my own good judgement, believed in myself enough to stand firm in differing opinions on our children when I felt David was too strict. Final pointers to couples entering marriage are: say your prayers together when you kiss and say goodnight, and **Do not go to bed angry. Make up** (even if it takes all night) — the next day will be brighter.

(CONTINUED ON PAGE 156)

Jane

*M*ost important has been advice given to me by my mother when Jane and I were married: "Never go to sleep angry at each other." Long ago I told this to Jane, and we both have been good in practicing this wise suggestion.

In addition, I try to avoid controversy by performing some activities that I do better than she does. As a result, since my retirement over a decade ago I have been making our bed, doing much of the dish washing, and (until the last year or two when declining physical strength interfered) doing almost all of our food shopping.

I try to be considerate, understanding and fair. I try not to be impatient about the excessive use of the telephone, but it sometimes has overwhelmed my efforts to suffer in silence. We both try to be cheerful and we create small surprises for each other that, when discovered, are attributed to "Gremlins."

I try to show and express my love and appreciation for all of her kindnesses, love and care. I am always truthful, open and hide nothing from her. I try to give praise where praise is due; and, fortunately for me, she is an excellent cook, which provides frequent opportunities for voicing my praise and appreciation of her efforts.

We try to do things together as much as possible and our similar tastes permit us to enjoy opera and concerts and walking (for exercise) together. Until I broke a hip ten years ago, we also played tennis, skied and sailed together.

David

13

Norman and Claire Berenson

Married on June 25, 1944
Philadelphia, Pennsylvania
His age: 24   Her age: 19

Claire's girlfriend's boyfriend and Norman belonged to the same fraternity at the University of Pennsylvania. The girlfriend asked Claire if she wanted to go to a frat party, which Claire did. At the party, acting on his attraction, Norman asked Claire "May I have this dance?" — a prelude to his future question "Will you marry me?"

I believe the paramount ingredient for achieving a lasting marriage is the maturity, willingness and ability to compromise (and not necessarily 50-50). Since every individual is unique and each partner comes to the marriage with a different background, upbringing, and lifestyle, it takes hard work to be able to live together even when in love.

Other ingredients are trust, respect and the ability to communicate when problems arise, to deal with them and resolve them amicably. Also, the couple must adjust to life changes, i.e., career and job changes, children — birth and raising them, empty nest, and retirement. Adjustment must be made to different habits, interests, and extended families. And, very importantly, they must agree on how money should be spent.

I don't think there is any way of knowing what to expect before marriage — life is too complicated — so it must be a learning experience and keeping the commitment in mind which was made at the wedding.

Claire

*F*or true compatibility in a marriage, the partners should trust and respect one another. A level of intelligence that is similar is very helpful. Conversely, a diversity of personalities may help solidify the marriage, as checks and balances are needed.

If both parties take every incident very seriously, or too lightly, trouble is brewing. A balance is needed to smooth over any problem that occurs — e.g., two worrywarts on every little thing that comes up in everyday life may lead to disaster. One partner has to be able to comfort the other, and see the light side of occurrences. "A Devil May Care" attitude for both partners is just as bad. If neither one takes any responsibility of watching over their offspring, or are careless with their assets, a failure is probable.

The couple should be able to do their thing; have some private time from each other. However, they must also like many of the same things, must like to be with each other, converse with each other, and laugh together.

It is most important for the couple to always be at ease with each other. Lastly, the absence of any mental or physical abuse is a very necessary ingredient for a successful, long-lasting and loving marriage.

Russell and Ruth Blinick

MARRIED ON JUNE 20, 1952
CHICAGO, ILLINOIS
HIS AGE: 26   HER AGE: 24

Call it "Woman's Intuition." Russell's family was friendly with Ruth's sister-in-law's family. The sister-in-law had an inkling that Ruth and Russell would be an ideal couple. She set up the two on a blind date and the pair clicked.

Russ and I met at a time in our society when, if you married, it was to be permanent. We married when I completed my social work training and was starting a job in my chosen field. Russ had just evaluated what he wanted to do with the rest of his life after completing $3^{1}/_{2}$ years in architecture school. So he returned to undergraduate school, majoring in chemistry and working part-time while I worked full-time. He graduated in June 1954. These early years were so good because we had common goals and not much money and our creativity went a long way.

We started our family when we were 28 and 30. I feel that we were mature and settled in our relationship. We have two daughters whom we are very proud of. They are so different and individual, and they care about the world they live in and each other. They are certainly part of the bonding between Russ and me!

It took us many years to learn how to "fight" but now we are aware that we have periods of stress, can argue, get it out on the table and negotiate it, and then let go of it! A sense of humor is always important! Having common interests (golf, bridge, and people) is basic; yet we have outside interests that we each pursue. Mutual respect is very important. I feel young people today have had so much provided for them materially, that they do not have an opportunity to develop their own inner strengths. The society is a "throw away" one and Hollywood helps support that instant satisfaction is the way to go. With that as their core, how can people survive the realities of living together and working together and problem-solving?

Ruth

I believe that beyond the initial attraction between the two of you, a commitment to the permanence of the relationship is paramount. There are many wonderful "ups" and difficult "downs" in the course of a long marriage and certainly moments of wanting to flee. There slowly evolves, however, a realization that something strong and reassuring is being established. Sharing your life with someone else is certainly not easy and should not be expected to be so. Coming from different backgrounds creates different expectations and most certainly creates initial clashes. Communicating, therefore, becomes vital. The understanding that evolves is truly remarkable. It's a little like a chamber music ensemble…an unspoken understanding of an approach to situations that almost requires no conversation. Certainly common interests, i.e., outdoor activities, theatre, music, etc., should be exploited; they are part of the glue in the relationship. There is a joy in mutual delight. Conversely a certain amount of exclusive activities by both parties contributes to the richness of the relationship. Finally, and certainly personally, having children is a magical experience that does not diminish with time. To the contrary, watching the struggles and blossoming is a magic all its own. In summation, it's impossible for me to imagine a different path taken.

Russell

Conley and Irene Blough

MARRIED ON NOVEMBER 28, 1946
HOLLSOPPLE, PENNSYLVANIA
HIS AGE: 23   HER AGE: 22

God Bless the USA! Stationed in Bolton, England during his service in the US Air Force, Conley went to a local dance one evening for some fun and socializing. There, he was introduced to Irene by mutual friends. Love bloomed.

*I*ngredients for a good marriage: Kindness, Implicit Trust, and Respect and Acceptance of each other and each other's talents.

My husband and I never argue about money — however, there was always honest and open communication about it. I was the family accountant and my husband always supported me. How very important this was!

Loving touch — we always held hands and still do. It was very important to me to be able to touch my husband and have him respond. He has never let me down.

Acceptance of each other's imperfections — no one is perfect!

Good humor — be able to laugh, especially at yourself.

I am grateful to my mother and father because they had many troubles but still supported each other. They taught me that we can surmount just about anything if we know that we can depend upon our loved ones.

I cannot think of anything that would have prepared me for marriage — it is a unique experience. For me it was the best decision I ever made.

Irene

I will list a few items that I think are some reasons our marriage has lasted close to 60 years:

1. We never argued about money. Whatever we had was ours, not yours or mine. We rarely borrowed money and all bills were paid on time.

2. We had complete trust in each other.

3. Sharing came easily. Money, time and chores. All bank accounts and bills had both of our names listed.

4. We tried to be kind to each other and to other people.

5. We appreciated each other and everything we had.

6. Acceptance of imperfections in each other.

7. I think we needed each other — someone to love and to share our life.

I have never regretted marrying my wife. She is the best thing that ever happened to me.

Conley

Charles and Marjorie Bourne

Married on March 28, 1942
Cleveland Heights, Ohio
His age: 22   Her age: 24

A church meeting to start a new youth group also created a courtship. Majorie and Charles met at an organizational get-together. When the gathering concluded, Marjorie asked around for a ride home. Charles gladly accommodated. Hallelujah!

As we look back on our marriage, we realize that our Lord brought us together. I was new in Cleveland, and went to my sister's church on Sunday night to meet people. Charlie offered to take me home, and I had to ask him his name! We were married six months to the day in the same church. As I walked down the aisle, I thought to myself, "This is it!!!" This was 1942, and World War II was facing us. Our Lord had a plan for our lives. Of course we've had our troubles, but He has always taken care of us. Charlie and I didn't always agree, but we talked it over, **never** saying anything bad, **never** an angry word, and he has always been the head of our family. We really love each other, and try to take care of each other. The 23rd Psalm has been our lifesaver.

Marjorie

When I met my future wife in church, I had no way of knowing that this pretty, petite blonde would become my bride six months to the day later in the same church. This was the beginning of a marriage as "heirs together in the grace of life."

We had our troubles early on as my bride soon developed pleurisy and was bedridden for six weeks, and I was laid off when the company switched from making sewing machines to war products. We were fortunate that I was deferred from the draft for six months. In spite of these early troubles, we shared a bond that enabled us to "weather the storm" with God's help.

My advice to young people — married or about to be — is to make a commitment that your marriage will always come first, and your love will grow stronger. Learn to do things together and enjoy each other's company.

Charles

Helen and Oswald Bronson

Married on June 8, 1952
Tampa, Florida
His age: 24   Her age: 26

In Sickness and in Health: Helen and Oswald met at Bethune-Cookman College. During his senior year, Oswald became ill and was hospitalized for a year. Helen routinely visited, helping him keep a positive frame of mind. After recovering, she took him to the bus station to return home. Flash! They realized they had fallen in love…and Oswald proposed right then and there!

*O*ur marriage has been a wholesome experience filled with numerous high moments and penetrating challenges. These high moments and challenges relate to communication issues from the birth of our children to their graduation from college. These high moments also included our involvement in each other's graduation from college and graduate studies as well as my husband's several vocations.

It is reassuring to state that my husband respected me as a full partner in our marriage. By the same token, I gave him my full support in his successful vocational pursuits. It is essential that couples learn to cooperate as **equal** partners in terms of the talents and abilities that each brings to the marriage.

We constantly arranged to spend time alone which afforded us the opportunity to nourish our marriage with romantic experiences necessary to survive the monotony that creeps into all personal relationships. We also used these moments alone to make plans for our future and that of our children.

We have made efforts to understand each other prior to reaching conclusions regarding what is being said in our conversations or in our non-verbal communication. I do not mean that there were no misunderstandings, but that every effort was made to heal any misunderstandings through factual communication and heartfelt and loving listening. (CONTINUED ON PAGE 156)

Helen

*O*ur 50-plus years of marriage have been made possible and fulfilling by several factors. First, there was genuine love for each other. This love was more than the sensual or sexual aspects of a successful marriage. It was a love energized by deep respect for one another. This respect led us to consider each other's views in making decisions regarding financial matters and in our overall planning for our future. We, therefore, agreed not to take each other for granted.

This mutual respect mentioned above readily grew out of the religious orientation that we both brought to our marriage. This orientation enabled us to revere each other as "sacred" human beings — a sacredness that comes from our existence as creatures of a Divine Creator. We felt that we sin against God when we disrespect each other since we came into being by God's Divine Mandate.

Secondly, this theological orientation helped us **not** to see each other as an **it** or a **thing** or **object** to be manipulated or used for one's own ego satisfaction. Rather, we learned to view each other as persons equipped with brainpower, and emotions fully capable of making effective contributions to the marriage.

Thirdly, we learned the importance of fully "listening" to each other before rushing to conclusions about what the other is seeking to communicate. (CONTINUED ON PAGE 157)

Oswald

Alvin and Shirley Bush, Jr.

MARRIED ON MAY 24, 1951
BELLEVILLE, ILLINOIS
HIS AGE: 23 HER AGE: 21

Time was ticking away. Neither Alvin or Shirley had a date for an upcoming dance sponsored by a youth group to which they both belonged. Alvin's friend was taking Shirley's friend, and the friends devised a solution. They introduced Alvin and Shirley, who became ideal partners on and off the dance floor.

I have found 14 things listed below to be contributing factors in our long and happy marriage. These are things that I would suggest any young couple consider to make their life together a long and a happy one:

1. I gave husband freedom to pursue his intellect.
2. He was a terrific teacher of children through jobs around the home, from finishing the basement to working on cars, etc.
3. Being faithful to my husband.
4. Introducing the children to religion and its importance.
5. Understanding health problems and keeping the family healthy.
6. Seeing my husband's temper on very few occasions and realizing I needed to rethink my statement or the existing problem.
7. My seeing that we ate three good meals a day and maintained healthy bodies.
8. Being able to enjoy the travels that were not possible during the years of raising three children and caring for two grandmothers who died in our home, one with Alzheimer's and one who died at age 93.
9. Before marriage, trying to understand what the word "love" meant.
10. Enjoyment of antiquing and collecting with my husband.
11. Allowing my husband time to pursue his computer hobby wherever it takes him, and his hobby working on clocks.
12. In his working days, being so proud of his accomplishments in missile and space programs.
13. His allowing me freedom to come and go and do things I enjoy.
14. We are both only children and perhaps that was a plus for our marriage in understanding each other.

Shirley

L ooking back over the past 50-plus years, I find that several elements went into making our marriage a wonderful experience. I had excellent role models in my parents and grandparents. They always showed the greatest respect and consideration for each other. Each parent carried out their obligations and responsibilities in sharing the work and joys of their marriage. With this image, I was looking, perhaps unknowingly, for someone who could share my life in a similar fashion. This is not something that you know right away. Various indications in the way a person acts and reacts to situations lead to your formation of an opinion about them. I chose a person who responded with a concern and consideration to my actions, my activities and myself. This made me feel a deep love and trust for her. She obviously had, and demonstrated, similar feelings for me. We have maintained these feelings and relationship throughout all of our years of marriage.

Such a lasting relationship can only be maintained if you are honest and truthful with each other, have trust in each other, recognize that each of you has faults that need to be accepted or modified, do not belittle or "put down" one another, are always considerate of the other's feelings and desires, provide each other with some free space to develop your own personal aspirations, and maintain your common goals and dreams. These things apply to a marriage whether it includes children or not. In a marriage with children, the demands are greater as are the responsibilities. However, the consideration for each other must be strong and dominant in order that the children receive the best care as well as examples of love, which they see you express for each other.

Alvin

Edmund and Bee Caine

MARRIED ON OCTOBER 17, 1942
NEW YORK, NEW YORK
HIS AGE: 30   HER AGE: 25

"Happy New Year!" has double meaning for Edmund and Bee. They were introduced prior to Christmas by Edmund's cousin, who attended the University of Alabama with Bee. Fast-forward one week to a New Year's Eve party where, together, Edmund and Bee watched the stars twinkle into the wee hours of the morning.

After more than 60 years of marriage, I always tell people "Time flies when you're having fun." Truly, my husband and I continue to feel like newlyweds and we are each other's best friend. We have had some hard times — financially, medically, and otherwise — but there has never been a time when we were not there for each other 100%. No day goes by that we don't tell each other "Love you." I don't want to give the impression that we always agree on everything; we talk out our differences and we compromise. We have had a few big quarrels, but loved each other more after we got it out of our systems. We have rarely gone to bed mad at each other. I strongly recommend a double bed. I think our marriage has been a success because of our senses of humor. We have weathered many a crisis through laughter. It helps that we have similar backgrounds and entered marriage with a commitment and determination to make it work.

We have been blessed with two sons, and they have returned our devotion. Their lives dominated our lives until they matured. Now we try not to be dependent on them but remain close.

Bee

Fate has played a great part in our lives. We had both moved from the South to New York City where we met through a cousin of mine who had been to college with my wife. Pearl Harbor was part of the Fate inasmuch as our first date came about when my wife's date with a soldier at Fort Monmouth was broken when all leaves for the post were cancelled. My date was also broken because the girl wanted to see her parents in California when war was declared. Bee and I got together New Year's Eve and thus started our romance, which resulted in marriage.

We are happily married and very active. We attend Senior University of Greater Atlanta twice a week, exercise daily, and I volunteer at Emory Hospital twice a month.

We love to travel and have been on seven continents and in more than 50 countries. We have faced the challenges of Antarctica, Africa, Australia, New Zealand, the Orient, Russia and China.

We attend sporting events, ballets, plays, concerts, and museums. Even if one of us has never attended a certain type of event, we make every effort to find out what attracts the other and we go together. Be flexible.

Long marriages are wonderful and the physical part should be kept up as long as possible. Finances are important and should be shared by both partners. Stay out of debt. Don't go to bed mad at each other. Be sure to say you love each other morning and night. Never allow your original family to interfere in your marriage. You vowed to "forsake all others."

Edmund

Michael and Lillian Capko

MARRIED ON DECEMBER 20, 1941
CHICAGO, ILLINOIS
HIS AGE: 21   HER AGE: 20

Just as Cinderella's glass slipper lured Prince Charming into her life, Lillian's hosiery brought Michael into her life. Michael worked for a department store. One day he waited on Lillian, who was shopping for hosiery. Michael helped her find the perfect fit, and consequently, both salesman and customer found the perfect fit for a lifelong mate.

Once we became Mr. and Mrs., our in-laws became our parents. My husband's parents, Alexander and Theresa Capko, became my mother and father. My parents, Alchimadonte and Gina Canalini, became my husband's mother and father. He could visit his folks any time, any day. The same for visiting my folks. That was fine with us both. That gave us a good start with our marriage. That is one reason our life is so good together and that made us very happy.

The next reason is the most important thing in our lives together, our children. They bring us happiness. Our love and happiness grows from all our children. These children are our life and love. While growing old with our children and children's children, we are growing younger. At least being with kids makes us feel younger and younger. There are ball games to go to and school performances. They come over to visit, swim and eat. They keep us busy and happy. We enjoy all of our family so much, I wish you could feel how much.

One other reason that I think has helped Mike and I over the years is that we go out almost every night to the same restaurant for coffee, but more so for talking. The servers all know us and call us Mah and Pah! If we miss a night, they become concerned. It is great to have this time together to sit across from one another and just talk and talk and talk. We talk about everything that happened that day, week or month. All of our children know where we are and sometimes will join us. If any of our children are over with their kids and coffee time rolls around, they encourage us to leave, so we do! They know how important this time is for us.

(CONTINUED ON PAGE 157)

Lillian

I met Lill when she, her sisters and other young ladies came in to buy Ladies Berkshire Hosiery at the men's clothing store I worked at in Chicago. This store was one block from a Catholic church. We were open on Sundays until one o'clock. After every Mass, a dozen or more women came into the store to buy hosiery. Since I was the newest help and the other salesmen would stay away, I was it. This was a plus because sooner or later these girls married and guess where they brought their men for clothes? Also guess who they wanted to wait on them? This was the start of over 40 years of my successful career in the men's clothing business. Better yet, it was the start of over 60 years of marriage to the girl I met selling women's hosiery to on those Sunday mornings.

In those days (the late 1930s) there were dances every Friday and Saturday nights. Lill and her sisters came to the dance on Saturdays and that was the night I attended. Seeing Lill and feeling like I knew her, I would ask her for several dances during the evening. After a period of time, we were dancing most of the evening together.

Dating came next. Lots of rules at the Canalini residence. Lill's only brother, Ray, had to talk to their parents to allow Lill to date me. After given the okay, we were given an 11 o'clock curfew. We would take a streetcar to a movie house a few miles away. Then after the movie, we'd stop at a soda shop. After three years of dating, Lill and I got married. I was making $18 a week. As a wedding gift, the boss gave me a raise to $25 a week.

In 1942, I was drafted and was gone for three years. Lill would follow me the times I was stationed in the states for awhile — Colorado Springs, California, and last in Durham, North Carolina. (CONTINUED ON PAGE 157)

Michael

Guy and Alice Chancey

Married on September 5, 1931
Tampa, Florida
His age: 23   Her age: 16

Walking and dancing are not only good exercise, they can be the route to amouré. Guy and Alice met initially when each was taking a neighborhood stroll. The two stopped, chatted a bit, and then went in different directions. Destiny reunited Guy and Alice a year later when they recognized each other at a local Moose Club dance.

Think about things that can happen after the marriage, such as are you really so much in love that you will be willing to work at marriage, good or bad? Remember he will be the father of your children.

Is he someone trustworthy you can depend on to make a living wage and your children will be proud of? Being a dad can be a long-lasting responsibility. Does he want children and will he take the time with children in play, sickness, and help to guide them in the right direction? If an argument comes up, do not both get angry at the same time — one of you laugh and make a joke of it. Remember your children will hear if you lived right. Family and friends talk a lot, make it good.

Alice

Understand each other. Really consider this commitment and make sure this is what you want to do. Talk over what you want in life and what you expect from each other. Make sure you have common interests and are compatible. How are you going to support a family? Discuss jobs/promotions which could involve a move. Will it effect each other, and are you willing to give or take for that other person? You want to love that person for the rest of your life and be ready to commit.

I wish I had known how to get a better education. Not finishing elementary school, I was lucky to be self-employed and made a very good living to support my family.

Guy

31

Sidney and Lillian Charschan

MARRIED ON JUNE 9, 1946
BROOKLYN, NEW YORK
HIS AGE: 23   HER AGE: 21

Like magnets, Lillian and Sidney were attracted while vacationing in the Catskills. Summer after summer, many of the same families lodged at the resort. All of the teenagers stuck together. Though they had an abundance of choices, Lillian and Sidney always gravitated to each other.

When I first met Sid I felt an immediate attraction to him and knew that I wanted to know him better. In spite of our youth we were able to talk easily, we had so much in common coming from the same background, including religion. We had the same family holidays, liked the same food, believed in God, and wanted to be together as much as possible, even though we tried dating others at that time. We were sexually attracted to each other but believed in getting married by a rabbi first.

We got married when Sid returned from overseas, fighting in the Battle of the Bulge. I spent every Friday night of those war years having dinner with his parents because I knew what they were going through. When either they or I got mail from Sid, we called each other and helped get through the fear we were experiencing.

We did have some lu-lu arguments about raising our children and money, but tried to cool off and tried to meet each other half way. Our marriage has been one of loving and caring for each other's feelings and compromising when necessary. I believe it is necessary to love each other, think alike most of the time, and be sensitive to each other's feelings. This is the basis for making a lasting, loving marriage. Make sure you get to know your mate before you jump into bed with him. Discuss if you want to have children and how you will raise them. Listen when your mate talks to you, and hopefully he will do the same. Understand each other without becoming possessive or jealous. You'll know if your marriage is working the way it should because you'll want to be with each other as much as you can.

Lillian

We met in the Catskills when Lillian was 15 and I was $17^1/_2$. At that time my family had moved from 40th Street in Boro Park to East 2nd Street in Flatbush four blocks away. It was close enough for me to ride over and take Lillian for a handlebar ride on Ocean Parkway. Living close by had its advantages.

Before I went overseas, we saw each other as often as feasible. Tried dating others, but always came back to my Lil Sweetheart. We did get married by a Justice of the Peace in Boston where I was shipping out to Europe in the Infantry. I wrote as often as I could while Lillian worked at the home front saving some money for our future together. She still has shoeboxes full of my letters and pictures.

We were married in Brooklyn by a rabbi in front of all our friends and relatives. Lillian supported me while I was going to Columbia for an Engineering degree, and we were living in our basement apartment in Sheepshead Bay.

My first job caused a move to Poughkeepsie, New York, close enough for frequent visits to Brooklyn because I appreciated the importance of Lillian's first move from family. Our family grew. Our son Bill and daughter Wendy were both born in Brooklyn, near the grandparents. Subsequent moves finally ended in Levittown, Pennsylvania, also within visiting distance. My job entailed frequent travel, and considering Lillian's and my feelings, I would call or bring her along whenever possible. We have seen much of the world together. (CONTINUED ON PAGE 157)

Sidney

Arthur and Anna Cohen

MARRIED ON JANUARY 20, 1951
NEW YORK, NEW YORK
HIS AGE: 27 HER AGE: 22

"Brotherly Love" triumphed! Anna and Arthur's brother were friends at Hunter College. The brother invited Arthur to a college party, which he attended— reluctantly. There, Arthur and Anna were introduced. The event Arthur grumbled about turned out to be a magical evening with his wife-to-be.

Ingredients? Ingredients will depend upon the taste buds of the participants. We all come from such different cultural and psychological backgrounds, needs, and education, that no pat formula would satisfy all couples — or even a majority. Put very simplistically — a sadist and a masochist might make a perfect pair. Extend both of those categories into a lighter part of their spectrums and you probably have the basis for many 50-year marriages!

Basically, ideally both should be able to change; to initiate change and anticipate change; and sometimes switch roles. Hope and pray (if suitable to the individuals) that there are no major random disasters to occur to either of them or their children. I'll bet many a marriage sailing along with glorious travel plans sunk on those hidden reefs.

Pointers? Be sure you are deeply in love — that helps, but look around. Many couples make it with only a lukewarm attachment in the beginning. Spend some married time together before having children. We did (nine years) but many don't and didn't.

Advice before marriage? A Catholic girl and a Jewish boy — do you think we listened?

Anna

Firstly, what follows is surely not meant to be exhaustive. I am responding at a moment in time. At some other time, be it another day, week, month, year, in another situation or set of circumstances, I may respond differently, at least somewhat differently.

So, with the above provision, I begin.

A long-lasting marriage demands loving, liking, and respecting. If I love, like, and respect me healthily, I will love, like, and respect thee healthily. It requires feeling, thinking, empathizing, and patience. One must be sensitive, sensitized, and yet be able to detach sufficiently so as to be cognizant of what is going on.

It helps to be able to express one's self well and to listen well. When an event occurs, we ought not to over-analyze. We take things out of context. We analyze too often. We hardly ever synthesize. We take things apart. We do not put things together again.

Balance is an important requisite. We ought to have some sense of what is important and what is unimportant, what matters and what doesn't matter.

And the other requisite — luck/chance need be on your side. I've always been in awe of the accident, i.e., matters we cannot, do not determine or control. Things happen, at times because of, at times in spite of.

For those about to get married — Do not over romanticize. Marriage is not the panacea. Marriage probably will not be problem free. Rather, be problem-aware. If and when problems appear, work them through. Sometimes these are easy, other times difficult. (CONTINUED ON PAGE 158)

Arthur

Paul and Barbara Collins

MARRIED ON JULY 2, 1948
MIAMI, FLORIDA
HIS AGE: 27   HER AGE: 18

They sat side-by-side in church, but dating was forbidden because Barbara was a mere 15 and Paul was 24. The church's Sunday school held a beach party. Since Barbara wasn't allowed to ask Paul, she invited a fellow closer to her age. Paul escorted the Sunday school teacher. By the end of the party, Paul and Barbara split from their dates and left together.

Basically I feel **Trust** and **Honesty** make a marriage lasting. What starts off as physical attraction, in time turns into a deeper, more meaningful love and relationship. As one matures, so should your perspectives. You set common goals and are willing to work together for them — assuming the responsibilities of rearing children, making plans for college educations, and caring for older parents. As you mature so does your love for each other, it grows and grows. You just can't imagine how deep and meaningful your love becomes. Marrying an older, mature man with his feet on the ground sure helps. Would I do it again? **Yes!** Would I change anything? **No!**

Barbara

First, let me tell you about my wife: Coming out of the service and back to my church, I met this shapely, blue-eyed blonde with an optimistic attitude and a personality second to none. Two years later we married and two years later twin girls and later a son came along whom she raised like second nature. I know our marriage has lasted because we met in church, where we were married and still belong, and our faith in God plus a serious commitment of our marriage vows. My wife has always had an optimistic attitude about anything that I wanted to do. I feel very fortunate to have a wife with her attributes and accomplishments: 30-years plus as a hospital volunteer, 30 years teaching Sunday school, being involved in the children's school and church activities, and planning our vacations and social outings. Last, I ask, who would **not** want a marriage like that to last?

Paul

George and Suzanne Concelman

Married on November 18, 1950

Pittsburgh, Pennsylvania

His age: 24   Her age: 21

George's date at the University of Pittsburgh's Student Union never showed. Rejected but relentless, George noticed an attractive student sitting alone. He walked over to her and inquired: "Would you like to have a Coke with me?" Suzanne welcomed his offer. Within seconds, George's love life turned from fizzle to sizzle.

We've been married 50-plus years and the only thing I wish I'd known from the beginning is that it would get better every year! Better and better and better! I feel very sorry for couples that are divorcing since the best is yet to come.

We got one piece of advice from the minister who married us and it is one we carried with us from the beginning and one that works. He told us that there is no such thing as a 50/50 marriage. A good marriage is 75/25— and both sides must give 75%. We both have tried to give more in all we have done and it works.

I love my husband, but more than that I like him. He is my best friend and we like to do things together — forget all the nonsense about opposites attracting. Couples do better if they have similar likes and dislikes and come from similar backgrounds and religions.

Laugh and the world laughs with you, cry and you cry alone is true not only in the world, but also, especially, in marriage. A sense of humor is the best thing you can bring to marriage, and it will help you face all the problems of everyday living. Nothing gets too serious if you can laugh at it.

My advice to couples ready to wed is first, be friends, second, love each other, and third, laugh with and at each other. The time will fly by before you know it.

Suzanne

It is my belief that contentment and satisfaction in one's life is dependent on a few key decisions one makes. One of those decisions (perhaps the most important) is who you marry. A successful, happy marriage begins with the right choice of a mate and the keys to that decision are compatibility and love.

It may sound trite or old-fashioned, but the choice of a mate is also the choice of a long-term friend. Such factors as religion, education level, socio-economic status, interests, ethnicity, and attitude toward life are all important. The common theme of having to work to make a long-lasting marriage is probably true, but eliminating areas of conflict before you start sure makes the job a lot easier.

My wife and I like to be with each other. We go to church together, go on vacation together, go shopping together. We have friends together, laugh together, and go to bed together. There are, of course, activities we do alone (there is no place for a woman in a barbershop quartet), but even these activities are a shared interest and lead to conversations about what we are doing.

One aspect of our marriage that wasn't planned or anticipated, but turns out to be important, was complementary skills and abilities. Such things as creativity versus detail orientation or cooking versus cleaning up. The net result is that everything gets done to our satisfaction without serious conflict.

Despite the concept of marriage common in books and movies, as a relationship of fight and make-up, in my mind compatibility and love are the keys to happiness.

George

Sydney and Rosalie Cooper

Married on November 15, 1942
Lake City, Florida
His age: 24   Her age: 21

Rosalie trailed along with her cousin and her cousin's date Sydney to a religious youth-group weekend. The cousin invited Sydney, a platonic friend, because her boyfriend couldn't go. During the weekend, Cupid's arrow struck Rosalie and Sydney.

I would tell a young couple to always speak to each other. Discuss all your plans and problems. Do not keep secrets. My husband and I never had to go to a "marriage encounter." We could always talk it out!! Be sure to remind each other that "I love you!" Have respect for each other's opinions. Give each other **space.** Try not to argue over money or children. Ours has been a wonderful and happy marriage.

Rosalie

*R*equirements for a loving, long-lasting marriage:

1. Mutual love for each other.
2. **Mazel** (good luck) in health, mental and physical.
3. Enjoy good humor and good sex.
4. Prudent financial stability.
5. In rough times, perseverance.
6. Have compassion, understanding and compromise.
7. Always allow your wife to win (she will anyway).
8. Make up your differences before going to sleep.
9. Be kind and thoughtful to each other's parents.
10. Listen to your children as much as possible.

Knowing all that I know for more than 60 years, it's better than being alone.

Sydney

Alan and Idell Corson

Married on December 21, 1947
Philadelphia, Pennsylvania
His age: 22   Her age: 20

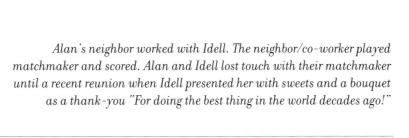

Alan's neighbor worked with Idell. The neighbor/co-worker played matchmaker and scored. Alan and Idell lost touch with their matchmaker until a recent reunion when Idell presented her with sweets and a bouquet as a thank-you "For doing the best thing in the world decades ago!"

*A*lan and I were married at a young age. We met after the war, dated and married in that order. Even though we were young, I feel the war years had given us a maturity that I see is lacking in today's couples. We rented an apartment for $43.38 a month — no kitchen sink (dishes were done in a pan and rinsed in the bathroom). It did have a garage even though we didn't have a car. With Alan going to school under the GI Bill and my working we made $205 a month; it didn't matter, we were deliriously happy. Several years later, we moved with our 18-month old son to a house that was 1,000 square feet and we loved it. Friends made our lives even better. We became very involved in the synagogue which satisfied our spiritual and social needs. But Alan changed jobs, which necessitated moving to Minneapolis. Once again the synagogue was a focus in our lives. We quickly became part of the community. College took our two children, and we moved again, this time to Washington D.C. Once again we were empty nesters — just as we started. Life is different when you move without children — but with our jobs and so much to see, we were happy. Since we've retired, we have done lots of volunteer work, which makes our lives full. Over the years we've had our ups and downs (luckily more ups than downs). But our love for each other has never wavered. We are happy and so grateful for good health and a good family. We haven't done everything right but we feel we've done more things right than wrong. I feel our dedication, patience, respect and, above all, our loyalty to each other is a big factor in our love, which is even stronger than it was when we married.

Idell

*O*ne of the primary requirements for a successful marriage is respect — respect of self and respect for your mate. Marriage has to be a union of equals. It's not important which one earns the most money. You need to live within your resources. We accepted what we had and were very happy with it. Most couples today do not take this approach, it seems. Our respect for one another carried throughout the raising of our children. I'm not sure that we were able to convey this to them although they seem to be doing O.K. We also tried to follow the trite expression — "don't go to sleep mad." It works. Also, I feel that marrying within our religion was a major plus; it's one less argument that can arise when there's a disagreement of any sort. It also provides a base for social relationships and the advantage of a spiritual counselor when needed. It certainly helped when we made a major relocation — to have a Jewish community and to develop a great set of **friends** with whom we still meet. It was a major strain on my wife — she wasn't thrilled with the idea of moving so far away from family but accepted my wish for a better opportunity. The job change didn't work out as planned, but the move outdid our wishes. She really made it work. Even today she still goes more than 50% of the way. She is my life and, I believe, I am hers. It just gets better and better.

Alan

Cary and Virginia Creamer

MARRIED ON NOVEMBER 24, 1948
LOUISVILLE, KENTUCKY
HIS AGE: 24   HER AGE: 23

Happy Homecoming: Cary's friend and Virginia's best friend were boyfriend and girlfriend. When Cary returned home from duty in the Marine Corps, the couple wanted to help him jump start his life. They arranged a blind- and double-date with Cary and Virginia. Their kind gesture worked.

We have lived long enough to see all our theories about what makes for a long and happy marriage proved questionable. We've seen couples that we thought would have a wonderful married life end up divorced and we've seen couples where we were sure that marriage would not last three years celebrate their golden anniversary.

We have been happily married over 50 years and in our case, the fact that we had a very similar background may have helped a bit. We were both raised in Louisville, Kentucky, lived about five miles apart (but never knew each other), our fathers were both traveling salesmen — in fact they both worked for the same company, we both attended the University of Louisville together and dated the whole time we were in college.

Another thing that makes it so difficult for us to give young people advice about married life is the fact that the world is entirely different than it has been during our lifetime. Nothing that our parents could have told us when we got married could have prepared us for all the changes we've seen. My father thought that if I ever made $10,000 a year we'd be rich — just one example of how difficult it is to give meaningful advice. Another example of change is the number of working mothers today compared to when we got married — I think the figure today is more than 50% compared to maybe 10% 50 years ago.

We believe some of the ingredients of a happy and long marriage would include shared values, commitment, responsibility, mutual respect, the ability to be forgiving, and a desire to please each other and love.

Shared values would include common aspirations for the children's education, money management, church support and church activities, social and recreational activities, etc.

Commitment means that each partner will strive to make the marriage successful no matter what the obstacles.

Responsibility means that partners carry out their agreed upon and accepted tasks in a responsible and dedicated manner.

Mutual respect means that each partner respects the other's opinions and idiosyncrasies no matter how crazy they may seem.

The ability to be forgiving means that when one partner does something that hurts or annoys the other, he/she is generously forgiven.

A desire to please each other comes naturally from their love for each other.

Many of the above ingredients would also be important in other kinds of relationships such as business associates, best friends, political alliances, etc., but in a marriage the big difference is love — this is the unique ingredient in a marriage that can make all the others work so well.

AUTHORED BY CARY

Virginia   Cary

John and Edna Crowley

Married on November 20, 1943
Norfolk, Virginia
His age: 25   Her age: 21

Dating can be expensive, but John started emptying his wallet before dating Edna. Edna worked for a tobacco company. The company's office building had a lobby store and Edna covered for the store's clerk during lunch hour. John was an intentionally frequent customer as he inched his way into Edna's heart. Cha-ching! Cha-ching!

John and I have been involved in a very happy marriage for 60 years. Our life together has been one of great commitment, primarily to each other, with our children a loving and loved second. There has been joy; there have been hard days, but working together, with a strong faith in God, we've come along just fine.

In the three (almost) years we dated before our marriage, we got to know each other very well. Ours was a "war marriage," with the first few years, years of separation and letter writing. I envy the newlyweds today, who are with each other from the day of their wedding, and can set up housekeeping immediately. We had to wait a few long years, so maybe that is why it was so very special and precious to us.

We enjoy being together. When we hear complaints about marriage partners, we wonder what has happened to what started out as a "real love affair"! Are people not willing to work at something that has such great potential for such wonderful returns?

When people start raising a family, they find it is not easy. Some days, it is downright difficult, and priorities can get mixed up for a time. We were able to have time, just for ourselves, away from the pressures that all families have. Our children knew — and know — how much they were — and are — loved. We all had our parts in building a happy family, and, as our family has grown, we see much of us in our children. They are good people, working with spouses, and committed in their marriages. We are proud and we are blessed.

Edna

To accomplish a long, lasting, and loving marriage I feel certain ingredients are definitely involved. The most important are:

A. **Luck or Good Fortune:** Edna and I became acquainted in 1941. We were both single and non-committed.

B. **Personalities:** We were both attracted to each other. We enjoyed each other's company and a close friendship blossomed quickly.

C. **Upbringing:** We discovered that we had much in common. We both had strong faith in God, and actually, many of our dates involved church activities. Unlike youngsters today, neither of us had an automobile. We both worked in Boston, and spent our lunch hours together. Edna was an urbanite and I was a suburbanite, so traveling to and from dates was easy, but a labor of love.

D. **Maturity:** Consistent with the Depression years, we grew up fairly quickly. Also, we were affected by World War II. We were separated for nearly three years. Our faithfulness to each other during this period strengthened our love and helped us to mature.

Edna and I have been truly blessed and have enjoyed 60 years of married life together. We raised a family, which we found was not an easy responsibility. We are proud of our family. All of our children grew up realizing right from wrong. How lucky we have been!

John

George and Ruthanna Davis

MARRIED ON JANUARY 25, 1936
EAST ORANGE, NEW JERSEY
HIS AGE: 25 HER AGE: 23

My marriage to George has been a joy. He is loving and generous and it is easy to talk things over with him. We seemed to have the same standards and expectations when it came to raising our six children. Perhaps we were a bit firm with our children. If my husband told one of them they couldn't do something—they knew it would be the same answer from me, even if I did not know what he had said. We always knew where they were and who they were with. When I called them in from play with my peculiar yodel, if they were slow in coming I said they were too far from home. They needed to come in by 5 p.m. from play. There was always homework, music to practice, baths to take, etc. We had no trouble with drugs, drinking, etc. We always took them to church with us and they are active to this day with the exception of one son who married a Catholic. Be honest, loving, generous and talk things over with your spouse. George is easy to love. I am very happy with him. I give him all the credit.

Ruthanna

In many ways marriage is like a tender plant. It requires constant nourishment and care if it is to prosper and bloom. It means that the marriage partnership requires daily care. The partner needs to be told daily how my love for her is constant. Her welfare and happiness is my constant concern. Since the common welfare is an object of the marriage, there is no room for fighting. It helps to have common standards but it is love of the partner that is a primary basis for decisions. If there are secrets, they must be to bring joy when revealed. Family finances must be understood by both partners and spending limited to income. It is well to remember that we need divine care and to give thanks on a daily basis.

George

Edward and Maxine Egan

Married on July 2, 1949
Chicago, Illinois
His age: 20   Her age: 18

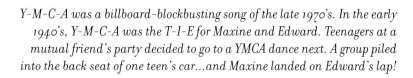

Y-M-C-A was a billboard-blockbusting song of the late 1970's. In the early 1940's, Y-M-C-A was the T-I-E for Maxine and Edward. Teenagers at a mutual friend's party decided to go to a YMCA dance next. A group piled into the back seat of one teen's car...and Maxine landed on Edward's lap!

We are all such individuals and life is full of events that shape our world and our relationships. When we married at 18 and 20 years of age, I was very immature and oblivious to my upcoming responsibilities. Ed had lived a life beyond his years, a dad who drank and abused him, a mom (child-like), and three sisters and a brother who at times were supported by him. He grew up fast. I attended an exclusive girl's school because we lived three blocks away. I met Ed when I was a freshman, got engaged in my junior year, graduated in June, and married in July. All the aunts thought I was pregnant because we were so young. Two years later I delivered a beautiful daughter, had a son in 1955, and our baby girl in 1957. Ed and I worked hard, and we scrimped — my parents helped us. We bought a house and our kids grew up going to Catholic schools. Ed and I had hard times — not much money, but through all our experiences we remained best friends. He was and is my helpmate. We've had a close family and our children are so good to us. They paid off our mortgage when we were married 44 years. (I raised them right!) We now have four grandchildren.

Maxine

We were so young, but so in love. What we did not know about the real responsibilities of life would fill a large box. With very little money to start out, my beloved and I slept in her family's living room till we found an apartment. I can remember our first purchases together — a blue dinette set with four chairs and a blonde four-poster bedroom set. The dinette set is long gone, but we still sleep together in that four-poster bed. During our great adventure, my beloved has presented me with three wonderful children. Their stories are unbelievable. Like all other humans, we have had problems and crises. We handled them together, as we did with all major decisions affecting the family. Socially we are different but we try to share each other's activities. Emotionally we are the same, often having the same idea at the same time. We still love each other, but best of all we are friends, and respect each other's abilities. Love and live the adventure, and follow our adopted prayer First Corinthians Chapter 13.

Edward

Morrie and Edyce Ellis

MARRIED ON SEPTEMBER 3, 1948
CHICAGO, ILLINOIS
HIS AGE: 23   HER AGE: 18

The corner drug store was the hangout for neighborhood teenagers: Edyce and her girlfriends would scope out handsome men; Morrie and his buddies would carouse for beautiful ladies. One day their eyes locked, and Edyce and Morrie have forever been entwined.

I have no idea what makes for a long-lasting, loving marriage. As for long-lasting, many friends in my age group have reached the 50-year mark. I'm sure many of us have thought of divorce. The reasons do not matter. When you have children it may be financially impossible to live apart. Time and effort by both partners help to sort things out.

Love is important but changes with the years. Every couple expresses their love in different ways. Your husband doesn't have to be lovey-dovey mushy to express his love. After 50-plus years you just know.

Couples getting married today are older and more set in their ways. They should be sure they can live together. It can be his place, her place or their place. One thing to remember: If your boyfriend has a few habits that annoy you, take my word for it, they get worse as he gets older.

I've been married so long that I can't think of anything I wish I knew before my wedding day. One thing I do know. It hasn't been a bed of roses but it hasn't been hell either. So I guess I'll keep him around for another 50 years.

Edyce

Wedded Blisters

Marriage is based on a contract and from its inception it should be conducted as all well-intentioned corporate enterprises. "Corporate" is the operative word because contrary to the common "partnership" belief: Mrs..., your "CEO," will make the crucial decisions in your marriage.

Your marriage (corporation) will be directed by an inexperienced taskmaster and even though she may create a seemingly insurmountable series of problems, fear not! The solution to your dilemma can be summed up in three simple words "minimal voice communication."

The Trappist monks, whether they are Benedictines or Cistercians, are generally thought to take a vow of silence. Actually, they do not take a vow of silence, but on the other hand they don't say much either. This fact, their almost total silence, is considered to be the single most significant issue contributing to the fact that there has never been a report of a Trappist divorce.

Silence is golden, do not speak unless your CEO insists, and she certainly will insist. When your CEO is expecting a response you must incorporate in that response, the simple words "Yes, Dear" in addition to any other words you decide to mumble.

To review, the prospect for a successful marriage can be enhanced based on the male's ability to implement a state of "minimal voice communication." Also, the words "Yes, Dear" should be included when you are obligated to respond to your CEO.

These two phrases, "minimal voice communication" and "Yes, Dear," plus a little luck could get you to the big 50.

Morrie

Ron and Joan Farrar

Married on October 22, 1951
Las Vegas, Nevada
His age: 26   Her age: 21

A passion to help those in need charted the course for personal passion. At UCLA, Ron was a member of a veteran's organization and Joan belonged to a service club. The two groups shared office space, so Ron and Joan often bumped into one another. While getting acquainted they discovered common interests, including each other.

The only thing I can definitely say from my own point of view, which certainly doesn't hold true for today's young people, is learn all you can about sex. Although Ron was well-versed in the sex act, when I married I hadn't even seen a naked statue of a man or known anything about what the sex act was or how it was done. Today's men and women are not so handicapped.

Ron and I came from opposite backgrounds, socially and culturally. His family was conservative Baptist and mine was Jewish. His parents and their families were for the most part white-collar workers while mine were professionals — doctors, lawyers. His parents rarely had words — they saved their disagreements and solved them privately. Mine were always fighting and very vocal about it. We often saved our grudges for days and let them fester until they burst.

Our first five years were extremely hard. He would walk away from disagreements and I would get into my car and drive for hours until I calmed down. At no time, however, did it ever cross our minds that divorce was the answer. We solved most of our problems by compromising. We'd each give a little here and there, and in the end harmony would be restored.

Eventually we found that we worked very well together as a team. We each had areas of life at which we excelled, or were especially good at. When we teamed up we found that we could do anything together, from raising our family to home maintenance, sports and supporting each other during the times we each sought higher education degrees.

(CONTINUED ON PAGE 158)

Joan

It is not difficult to ascertain the reason for the success (in terms of longevity) of the marriage of Joan and me. She didn't give up on me. I came into this relationship with a lot of excess baggage; I tended to do things my way at the beginning with little thought of what her preferences were. I was really a pill that she was forced to swallow. In my family, we never had arguments or fought over things; it was a calm but sometimes strained atmosphere. The only overt action that I remember was when my father chased me out of the house and around the block for doing something ungentlemanly to my sister — at least I think that was the reason. In Joan's family, (or so I'm told by her) there were constant arguments and fights — which is probably the healthy way to get something out of your system. I never fought with her or even argued vigorously. I remember losing my temper once — when we were in Nigeria setting up a school and curriculum. I remember yelling, "This is something I can't put up with!" But I forget now what that something was.

The secret of a long marriage is, I think, a very tolerant member who knows that the bad behavior seen will be mitigated somehow. I was selfish — perhaps insensitive is a better description. Many women, at least in these days, would have picked up and left in Joan's position, but for us, divorce was never an option. Our parents, I'm sure, would have been utterly dismayed if either of us selected it, as we would have been. One doesn't go that route — you work things out and if one of the partners has to suffer a little more, it still is not a separation-type of situation. My wife has only one problem — she undervalues herself. (CONTINUED ON PAGE 158)

Ron

Andrew and Renée Flager

MARRIED ON FEBRUARY 5, 1950
NEW YORK, NEW YORK
HIS AGE: 20   HER AGE: 20

They were neighbors and schoolmates for years. In high school, Andrew escorted Renée to the senior prom. The enchanted evening transformed their relationship from friendship to courtship.

We have always had a strong, absolute determination to make our marriage succeed, no matter what!

Pointers: Not every comment requires a response. Don't criticize each other's parents — ever! Focus on your mother-in-law's positive qualities; be especially nice to her. Apologize quickly if you are in the wrong. Acknowledge husband's help (even if it's just doing the dishes). Pay **sincere** compliments frequently. Don't discuss sensitive subjects before dinner — eat first! (My husband is very irritable when hungry). If you really want something, ask for it. Do not depend on hints or your husband's mind-reading ability. Also recognize that any characteristics disliked before marriage will remain after marriage.

Renée

There are many ingredients for achieving a long-lasting and loving marriage. Three of them are:

1. Be your spouse's best friend.
2. Do not be too judgmental.
3. Always be monogamous.

Joel and Margaret Fleet

MARRIED ON NOVEMBER 10, 1940
JACKSONVILLE, FLORIDA
HIS AGE: 24   HER AGE: 21

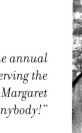

Joel and Margaret were waiting for the final segment of the annual High Holiday service to begin at synagogue. Both had been observing the traditional 24-hour fast. Joel's sister introduced them. Joel and Margaret still joke: "We were so famished, we would have fallen for anybody!"

ℛ ecipe For Achieving Long-Lasting Marriage:

Combine:

- 2 heaping cups of patience and cooperation

- 1 heart full of love

- 2 handfuls of generosity

- A big dish of laughter

- A whole lot of understanding

Sprinkle generously with kindness.

Add plenty of faith and mix well.

Spread over a period of a lifetime!

Enjoy!

Margaret

𝒥 ngredients for a long-lasting and loving marriage include having similar interests and being willing to adjust to any differences. Key pointer: Have patience. Understand that marriage is a question of "give and take."

Joel

Ernest and Lillie Fleming

Married on March 19, 1951
Deland, Florida
His age: 23   Her age: 17

The first day of school usually causes the jitters. For Ernest and Lillie, however, it was the luckiest day of their lives. On the opening day of junior high, the two were searching the rosters to identify their new class. Their names were on the same list, which led to an introduction. From that moment on, a friendship grew into an everlasting bond.

Marriage is one of life's richest and most rewarding adventures. Like a mutual pact, it involves the total personal commitment of two independent individuals to live as equal partners. Without this commitment, it becomes unfulfilling and empty. With the commitment, it becomes exciting and challenging. When a couple embarks on this lifelong journey, choosing to love, honor and cherish each other, before their immediate world, they are agreeing to utilize their combined strengths through tenderness, discipline and will to support, respect and love each other regardless of conditions or circumstances. When this is done, what was entered as a mutual partnership, through the years, will turn into a single union.

This is not to say that the adventure will always be a smooth, uphill journey. There will be many curves and potholes to interfere with the original commitment but love will enable them to stay the course. And each step along the way, whether painful or joyful, will be an occasion to cherish and celebrate.

Love must be the sure foundation on which to build a happy marriage. Longevity in marriage comes first of all from making your spouse your friend, someone who can be trusted, who will patiently understand the faults and imperfections of each other and love you just the same. When children become a part of the family, don't fall into the trap of devoting too much time and energy in them. Remember to leave some quality time for each other. Agree on the family principles and values you want to instill in your children making it emphatically clear that unity exists among both parents regarding choices made.   (CONTINUED ON PAGE 158)

Lillie

I knew in the 7th grade when I first saw my companion of more than 50 years that she was the love of my life and that my love for her would be eternal. Marriage is a partnership, a relationship between two people who share totally in a common enterprise for each other. This enterprise, like any well-run business, bases its foundation on **trust, confidence** and **respect**. When these commodities are included in some marriages, time passes swiftly and the relationship grows and flourishes into a wholesome relationship that neither time nor conditions can sever.

There have been through the years many roadblocks…times when money was short…advice from others plentiful…and careers were being developed. Yet, we were able to keep the lines of communication open and surmounted the obstacle that we faced one step at a time. At no point in our marriage were we ever a separate entity. We brought the partnership concept to the marriage and we have maintained it throughout. Disagreements sometimes surfaced but we were able to weigh advantages versus disadvantages and resolve the situation for the betterment of both of us without either party compromising their integrity.

I'd advise a couple embarking on the lifelong commitment of marriage to first of all know himself/herself as an individual. Know who you are and what your objectives in life are and how you can achieve them with a partner who can multiply your joys and divide your frustrations and griefs. Young couples must also know that in a partnership…there must always be positive investments of **love…loyalty…ambition…**and **energy** which will bring a vast amount of happiness and marital success.

Ernest

Leon and Louise Fradkin

MARRIED ON MARCH 25, 1948
PHILADELPHIA, PENNSYLVANIA
HIS AGE: 28   HER AGE: 20

Louise's long, flowing hair, sparkling eyes and radiant smile enamored Leon. Louise was hosting a party at her home. Leon was Louise's friend's date. He was captivated by Louise's beauty when she opened the door. In conversation, Louise and Leon realized they had many of the same interests. So, they set a date to get together again...and again...and again...

I was fortunate in having been raised by parents who were happily married, affectionate, loving people who were also very concerned that their two daughters were well educated and able to support themselves financially.

We have been married more than 50 years, and as I look back over all those years I don't remember any real conflicts. We both have similar interests, frames of reference and, for the first 15 years of marriage, almost similar careers. We were friends first, shared a similar college education and cultural interests. I feel that being friends helps a marriage. We both have always gotten along with one another's family and are both very family oriented with a strong sense of responsibility towards all family members. We have been jokingly accused of carrying kinship very far down the line.

We both have a sense of humor and appreciate each other's humor. Humor helps you get over rough times, conflicts with raising children and caring for older relatives. It also helps one to be able to put things into perspective. Very early in our marriage we made a pact never to go to bed angry and have abided by this all these years.

We still like one another, enjoy being together and doing things together even if it is only cleaning the windows. We are blessed with three children who are married to very nice spouses and 11 grandchildren who have enriched our lives. While our interests have grown in different directions over the years, we have always been supportive of one another and proud of the other's accomplishments.

Louise

*T*o understand why we are married over 50 years and aiming for 60, you have to understand why we married in the first place and how the elements that committed us to bond have managed to stay intact. I married because the biological inner pressure had reached a level in me that fear of marriage was overcome. I feared marriage because the idea of having to be singularly responsible for the welfare and safety of another human being — when I was not sure if and how I would be able to support myself seemed like a tremendous risk.

I decided to marry because I felt that being alone made my world a lonely one. I had plenty of friends and activities but I did not feel complete. I wanted the comfort of bonding with a woman. The comfort of sharing my thoughts and problems with a wife. The satisfaction that I was needed and that I had value. The idea of children and family did not become part of this equation till years later.

In Louise I found the answers to all my needs. She was someone to whom I could talk easily about the interests of my early years — art, architecture, music, and my belief in Zionism. She always made me feel welcome to her side of the marriage bed. She made me happy. She was there to comfort me when life's little disasters threatened me. In an unselfish way she made life for me a much easier road to travel.

I have tried my best to do the same for Louise.

But how does one keep the glue that bonds the marriage from coming apart? The answer is somewhere in keeping the couple happy and content more often than not. (CONTINUED ON PAGE 158)

Leon

Carl and Frances Fulmer

Married on December 31, 1939
Seminole, Florida
His age: 25   Her age: 25

It was in Mrs. Roberts's third-grade class that Carl and Frances developed a crush on each other. They exchanged their first kiss in tenth grade during a hayride. Childhood sweethearts evolved into eternal companions.

I believe a couple should have a deep and abiding love for the person they want to marry. They must be trusting and considerate of each other. You need to be compatible and go 50-50 in everything you do. It can't be "my money" or "your money" — it is now "ours."

Listen to each other when you talk. Don't hesitate to give compliments on things you do for each other. Plan little surprises for your mate and don't forget their birthday and other important dates.

Know how to cook and prepare good, healthy meals. Learn how to sew on buttons and mend rips and tears. Doing the laundry is a "must job" and ironing must be done. Keep your home neat and clean.

Know how to handle money and buy groceries. There are so many things the two of you do can do together to have fun.

In closing I would like to say — never go to bed angry, kiss good night and good morning, show and tell your mate how much you love him and appreciate him each day. This will make your wedding vows grow stronger day by day.

Frances

T he first thing you should know is all about the person you are going to marry. We were in third grade together, and we were sweethearts during school and we still are. During this period we learned about many things — each other's feelings, moods, love, helping each other and what it would mean to get married and have children.

We married and I had $75 in the bank and a job paying $75 a month. At this point we decided there was no "my money" or "your money." It was "our money." After more than 60 years, it is still "our money." We always saved the money before we made a purchase. We never charged anything, except to finance a car. We always planned our recreation and entertainment and did things together.

For a successful marriage, there has to be love, respect, consideration, harmony, agreement and lots of mind reading. We start each day with a hug and kiss and the same at bedtime.

Remember — There is no "my money."

Remember — No going to bed "mad."

Remember — Don't forget morning and night "hugs and kisses."

Carl

Hugo and Dorothy Gensicke

MARRIED ON AUGUST 4, 1945
PUEBLO, COLORADO
HIS AGE: 26   HER AGE: 25

Good things come to those who wait... A group of friends, Hugo and Dorothy among them, liked to jointly do various activities — attend religious youth group outings, gather at the grocery store hot spot, and rollerskate on Saturday nights. Over the natural course of time, Hugo and Dorothy developed a mutual adoration.

Using the word "Cherish":

C — Commitment and Cherish your husband.

H — Hear and listen to each other.

E — Erase all disputes. Don't carry a grudge.

R — Rely on each other in all areas.

I — Interest in activities of each other and also keep your individuality.

S — Support and share all responsibilities.

H — Have many happy moments.

Going from "me" to "us" is a tremendous adjustment. It is worth it.

Avoid overuse of credit cards.

In marriage, there will be peaks and valleys and all will be just great.

We survived the World War II era. I as a civilian working as an electrician in B17's and B29's, a period of time when women learned different jobs. A time of being independent. My husband was a veteran of five years in the Army Air Corps. Courtship continued via airmail and a few furloughs. We learned the basic rule for upheaval living at this time in history.

Dorothy

Take one day at a time. Trust each other. When we got married, people had a different attitude toward marriage. They believed it was forever and were willing to work as hard as necessary to make it work.

Don't make important decisions without consulting each other. Don't run up credit card debt. Keep separate bank accounts. Don't expect to change your spouse.

I can't think of anything I wish I had known before entering matrimony. I've never been expected to or tried to figure women out.

Hugo

Jonathan and Gilda Gittleman

MARRIED ON DECEMBER 21, 1947
NEWARK, NEW JERSEY
HIS AGE: 21   HER AGE: 21

Three is not a crowd. In her early teens, Gilda visited her cousin in New Jersey during the summers. The cousin was a friend of Jonathan. The trio palled around. As the years rolled by, a special fondness grew between Gilda and Jonathan. In their older teens, romance blossomed.

Assuming that love is the basis of a good marriage, there are ways to overcome the trials and sometime hardships of a good, lasting marriage.

Try to see the partner's point of view without making him/her feel guilty.

Learn to compromise without either partner feeling he/she got a raw deal. When you love someone, you don't want to hurt him/her.

Your partner is not a mind reader. Say what's on your mind.

Discuss possible solutions to disagreements. Sometimes one partner may have to yield completely. Know when to let it pass and when to pursue a solution.

Do things you know will make your partner happy such as kindness to his/her family. Overlook what you perceive to be a slight (providing this is not all one-sided). Help with a problem, project, chore, etc. Pitch in.

Listen to your partner, his/her feelings, thoughts, and ideas with undivided attention. The T.V. can wait.

Show interest in everyday mundane things when your partner needs you to. Life isn't always exciting or interesting. Be aware of each other's needs and try to satisfy them.

Show appreciation. Praise your partner. Make him/her feel important in your life. Develop a relationship where kind criticism can be given — no offense taken.

Arguments should not be aimed at hurting your partner. Remember this is someone you love. (CONTINUED ON PAGE 159)

Gilda

Elements For A Long Marriage

I suppose, if a couple marries when very young, they don't really think about staying married for over 50 years. I certainly didn't; I didn't really think that I would live long enough to consider it a possibility. Today people don't seem to marry until they approach middle age. Maybe that's their insurance that the marriage won't last over 50 years.

In any event, I believe the necessary ingredients for a long-lasting marriage are few.

First, and perhaps foremost, the individuals must be willing to compromise, in other words willing to give up the instant gratification on which they may have been brought up and have gotten used to. After all, what's sauce for the goose is not always — and sometimes infrequently — sauce for the gander.

Second, is an unwavering respect for each other as a person. This helps to insure that when emotional conflicts arise, and they are unavoidable unless the couple is a pair of robots, they will either be resolved or they will fade in importance. It also helps to insure that closeness and affection will grow with time.

Third, and last is having children and making them feel that they are loved and supported. Having children provides delicious and powerful glue after they reach adulthood and are having a family of their own. This is particularly evident when you see your children making theirs feel loved and supported.

Jonathan

Louis and Thelma Goldberg

MARRIED ON JUNE 1, 1947
PHILADELPHIA, PENNSYLVANIA
HIS AGE: 22   HER AGE: 20

72 hours! This was the length of Thelma's and Louis's courtship! On a Fourth of July weekend, Louis was visiting his sister at her apartment, and Thelma was visiting her sister who lived across the hall from Louis's sister. Fireworks exploded when Thelma and Louis met. A whirlwind three days later they got engaged.

Total Trust! Sharing and caring for each other, through good times **and** bad times. Listening to each other's concerns. **Encouragement** when needed. Raising a family (four children) together. Sharing various activities for their care, home life, help during school years, and maintaining a close family spirit were some things that brought us all closer together. It seems that after more than 50 years of marriage we still find our daily lives full of new challenges and rewards.

There should be a quality of attraction unlike any other one has known before. That special feeling of comfort and "this is someone I really enjoy being with." There was no doubt that this young woman was one of the most feminine, wholesome, and lovely women I had ever met. I did not have to think about her many qualities, her appearance, her attitude toward me, or why I knew I loved her…she was that special person I wanted to spend my life loving and sharing. Thus:

~ It is imperative that there is love and capability with mutual attraction.

~ An undefined desire to please, help and live happily with your spouse.

~ Trust and sharing all emotions, events, things you need for daily living, with the ability (even desire) to communicate about everything at all levels. Never let any problem or discussion escalate into an impasse where neither of us is right or wrong, but we share the pleasure of resolving needs together!

~ Conceive and raise our family **together**. The concept is that each child is a wonderful gift to us to love and mold into the best and happiest of beings. Children should be happy.

~ For us, our life together has been a beautiful adventure that has given us an "American dream" come true. Our love keeps growing!

~ It helps that I was always able to make enough money for us to live comfortably and that we were both content (even happy) to budget ourselves within our income! (CONTINUED ON PAGE 159)

Casimir and Eleanor Gorecki

Married on July 6, 1939
Eldred, Pennsylvania
His age: 24   Her age: ~

Eleanor had a date with Casimir's friend. Her date set up Casimir with Eleanor's friend. The four double-dated. In a twist of fate, Eleanor and Casimir had a fabulous time!

*I*f ever a marriage should have been doomed to failure, it was ours. We did everything wrong to start with. We came from completely different backgrounds. We got married secretly right after I graduated high school and spent the next five years getting acquainted. As so many marriages today, our marriage was based on physical attraction.

In spite of all this, we have celebrated more than 60 years of marriage. I am probably one of the most blessed women in the world. My husband expresses his love for me every day, not only with words but attentiveness to responsibilities and affection. I know he will always support me in my endeavors and he lets me know he appreciates my efforts to please him, whether it is a good meal or a letter to his relatives. I know he will always welcome anyone I invite to our home and will always forgive my mistakes.

We have two adopted sons and two grandsons. He has set them all a good example by his faith in God, his decency, his honesty and his wonderful sense of humor, and his eagerness to help anybody and everybody.

We both try to be courteous to each other and others. Sometimes, I see this lacking in couples who have been married many years. We make it a point to keep ourselves attractive to each other each day. (I put on makeup and perfume even when I am not leaving the house and he always shaves.) I feel like he is the one I love the most and deserves **the best**.

We are in fairly good health and enjoy joking and laughing a lot. It is so important. (CONTINUED ON PAGE 159)

Eleanor

*S*ome of the things I think that have made our marriage work:

Respect for one another.

High moral standards.

Maintenance of home and property.

Discussing finances.

Be slow to anger.

Be pleasant to company.

Remember special occasions with flowers, etc.

Hug and **kiss** spouse before bedtime.

Make her feel special.

Always tell her how elegant she looks.

Being married changed my whole life for the better.

I **owe** all of this to my **wife**.

Casimir

Jack and Elaine Halberstadt

MARRIED ON JANUARY 5, 1947
PHILADELPHIA, PENNSYLVANIA
HIS AGE: 21   HER AGE: 19

Never, never give up…Philadelphia's YMHA was a hub of action. Elaine, a hostess at its USO canteen, fibbed about her age so she could go to the dances. Jack patronized the canteen and he, too, frequented the dances. He was smitten with Elaine, but she was hesitant. With great persistence, Jack finally persuaded Elaine to go on a date and, eventually, he captured her heart.

Jack and I met when I was 17 and a senior in high school and he was 19 and in the officers V-12 program in the Navy during World War II. When we married, we were so very young and we grew up together. In today's world it shouldn't have lasted. It never occurred to us that marriage was not forever.

We're examples that opposites do attract. Jack always had a strong personality and I'm more easygoing and relaxed. I think we made a good team in raising a family. I have more patience and in times of difficulties we learned to talk things out. We learned the importance of sharing feelings and being less selfish and giving each other the space "to do our own thing." Over the years I have become more assertive and Jack has mellowed.

We also feel it's important to schedule "fun" time into our busy lives. We both love to keep in touch with our children, grandchildren, and friends of many years.

Keeping active and busy has kept us young in body and spirit!

Elaine

A long-lasting and loving marriage has to be built on a bedrock of shared values. Elaine and I were both relatively young when we married and, as a result, were far from being mature. In a financial sense, we started from ground zero and in fact, we lived with her parents for about two years before our joint income allowed us to move into a modest apartment.

As individuals we were quite different. She was initially not very outgoing or assertive. I, on the other hand, was the opposite. We knew that we were interested in having children (we produced three) who we knew would be in need of education and care so that they, in turn, would become responsible adults. They turned into good people and have brightened our lives with five grandchildren.

Life, I feel, is a continuum during which one should continue to grow and change, both as an individual and as a couple. And, in his or her process of growth, each partner should give the other sufficient "space." Perhaps "togetherness" can be carried too far.

Jack

Forrest and Marcella Haynes

Married on March 25, 1940
Louisville, Kentucky
His age: 20 Her age: 18

Forrest's and Marcella's lives crossed when they entertained at a Chicago night club on New Year's eve. Forrest's band had a gig, which included playing the music for Marcella's dance performance. A few years later, they became a "duo" for life.

When we met, our feelings and attachment for one another were inevitable, and even though my parents objected, my feelings could not be changed. We were married knowing we would have difficulties because of the times we lived. Little by little, we overcame our obstacles and soon we were blessed by the birth of two daughters. We accepted our new way of life and considered our way of life was the right and only way. Through the efforts and beliefs of my husband, we acquired our first home and brightened the way of life for our children. Today they are happily married with children of their own.

We thank the Lord for guiding us and always being there. His constant love has given us strength throughout our lives.

Defining the word "love" is not easy. It requires a mental and physical attitude practiced every day of your life. In my boyhood days, I was a Boy Scout and believed in the 12 laws of scouting. I find these words very descriptive of a successful marriage:

1. **Trustworthy**…trusting in one another and adhering to your vows.
2. **Loyalty**…completely loyal to one another.
3. **Helpful**…in sickness and in health.
4. **Friendly**…enjoy life, make each other laugh.
5. **Courteous**…to each other, and especially among other friends.
6. **Kind**…in times of sadness and sickness…understand and share each other's emotions.
7. **Obedient**…lying and cheating has no place in the love of one another.
8. **Cheerful**…remember, a smile is a frown turned upside-down.
9. **Thrifty**…to be successful such as a home, car, etc., sacrifice may be necessary.
10. **Brave**…there may be times when bravery is necessary for self-protection but don't be foolish.
11. **Clean**…physically clean and mentally clean is a must.
12. **Reverent**…path of righteousness and believing in each other.

All the laws may be hard to follow but it can be done. If you have trouble in doing and believing just remember these three things:

…You are what you think.

…You are what you eat.

…You only get out of life what you put into it. This is our way.

Leon and Irma Horowitz

MARRIED ON NOVEMBER 5, 1950
BRONX, NEW YORK
HIS AGE: 25 HER AGE: 19

The spell between Leon and Irma was cast on New Year's Eve. Strangers to one another, both attended a huge, annual hometown party at a hotel in Richmond, Virginia. Gazing amidst the crowd, their eyes connected. For Leon and Irma, it was an instant attraction.

How did I know he was the **Right One**??

I suppose I made a very lucky guess; but maybe I also judged him against what I saw at home — my parents had a loving and devoted marriage for almost 65 years.

We have similar backgrounds: strong religious beliefs, though not necessarily strictly observant; strong moral values; and loving parents. My in-laws celebrated 50 happy anniversaries, too.

We, too, share love and respect for each other and say, "I love you" every day — and mean it! We kiss a lot, too! We're honest with each other — and we both had to have a good sense of humor. It oils the workings of every marriage! We've become tuned and sensitive to each other's feelings and preferences. I could count on him to be supportive when I wanted to go back to school for special courses or try a new hobby or eventually go back into the work force. I encourage his interests as well and applaud every promotion.

We parented as a team, our styles were caring and encouraging, and our four children are successful, happily married and our greatest pride and joy.

But mostly we simply enjoy each other's company and spending time with our best friend, reading, gardening, traveling and celebrating Jewish holidays with our children and grandchildren.

We've been very lucky and we thank God often; but we've both put great effort to make our marriage happy and fulfilling and we feel we've succeeded.

Irma

Our long and happy marriage can be attributed to the fact that it has been a team effort from the day we met. We have shared and continue to share everything we do. We still continue to tell each other how we feel about each other and show that feeling in everything we do. Fifty-plus years of saying "I love you" and kissing whenever it suits us, of having the same moral ethics, of sharing our religious feelings, our love of gardening, traveling, reading, et.al., have been the key to our joint venture. We are fortunate and grateful that we have been able to teach our four children the value of our ethics, and they, in turn, have taught their seven children these values. This has contributed to making our golden years truly golden.

Leon

Charles and Martha Hough

Married on December 15, 1945
Philadelphia, Pennsylvania
His age: 27 Her age: 22

A nursing-school classmate of Martha also was a hometown, former next-door neighbor of Charles. The mutual friend paired Martha and Charles on a blind date. If either was ailing from a case of loneliness, their friend prescribed the right antidote!

I wanted to be faithful to my husband. When disagreements occur, it's best to give in and talk about it after a cooling-off period. When the children were growing up, I tried very hard not to argue in their presence.

We didn't live together before marriage as my strict upbringing in a loving Christian home instilled in me the values I have lived by. My husband and I do not belong to a church, which I feel guilty about.

Know your joint income including investments and pay all bills in full every month, avoiding high interest rates. Don't depend on Social Security and pension for retirement income, start saving from the time you get married.

After dating on and off for three years, I was quite certain our marriage would survive.

Martha

*O*ne should have completed his educational program and have an adequate income with reasonable prospects of maintaining one's standard of living. While many marry with one or both still in school, I don't think it is wise to do so. We were engaged before our education process was complete but waited. I passed my state boards and my wife finished training and had her R.N. (registered nurse) before getting married. (I was First Lt. M.C.A.U.S.)

It is important to honor and respect one's parents but one must sever the apron strings when married. They (parents) should not and if they attempt to dictate policy they should be politely informed to M.Y.O.B. My in-laws were ideal in this. They visited but never dropped in unexpectedly. They were helpful but never dictatorial. While we had met each other's family, we didn't seek their approval for our engagement and/or marriage. (A wealthy uncle apparently did not like this and never gave us a wedding present. He was domineering and the end result is his children's marriages suffered.)

One errs, I believe, in marrying one's first and only date. It is wise to date various persons but when one marries one should be ready to settle down to one partner. Having an extramarital affair is not only morally wrong but can be and often is an economic disaster.

Finally, while togetherness is fine, absence can be beneficial. We usually do things together but frequently have gone separate ways. My wife took our daughter on two trips to Europe and at other times for vacations at a nice resort. (CONTINUED ON PAGE 159)

Charles

William "Bill" and Elizabeth "Nan" Hunter

MARRIED ON AUGUST 9, 1944
AUBURN, NEW YORK
HIS AGE: 23   HER AGE: 21

You could find almost anything at Woolworth's 5¢ & 10¢ stores — including a husband or wife. Bill and Nan worked for the same retailer after school and on weekends. He stocked inventory, she sold housewares. Their everyday chats transitioned from dating to engagement to marriage.

Before our wedding day, an older co-worker said to me "getting married is like buying a 'pig in a poke.'" I asked her to explain because I had never heard that quote. It seems that farmers brought young pigs to the auctions in sacks. You bought them sight unseen. When you got home, you did the best you could with what you got. Some were first grade, some were runts, etc.

So when I married I decided that I would do the best I could with our marriage. I can't say that I was **always** patient and understanding but neither did I expect the same from my husband.

Taking marriage vows meant **forever**. Now people seem to think you can exchange partners like cars. Perhaps they "fall in love with love." If that model doesn't please you, trade it in for another.

I guess I'm happy because my "pig in a poke" turned out to be the best of the litter.

Nan

It is difficult for anyone married more than 50 years ago to give advice concerning marriage to young people today. We were brought up under completely different conditions, economically, socially, politically, and morally.

Fifty years ago there was less mobility, slower lifestyles, closer family ties, fewer methods of communication, and less exposure to the world.

Some pointers for couples considering marriage today would include having a sense of humor, a discussion of common goals regarding money, size of family, and style of living.

Two people should know each other for at least a year, even longer, before marriage. Know your partner before marriage.

Bill

Roland "Bill" and Nancy Jones

Married on October 17, 1942

Wynnewood, Pennsylvania

His age: 26   Her age: 22

Nancy is 5'. Bill is 6'2". Due to their stature, they'd sworn off blind dates: Nancy inevitably got matched with men who towered over her while Bill inevitably got matched with women who barely reached his shoulder. One day, a desperate girlfriend called Nancy because a group of lieutenants was in town and one more female was needed for a fix-up date. "O.K. But this is the last time," said Nancy. And it was!

*W*hat makes for a happy marriage? After more than 60 years of living and growing together, hopefully I might have some helpful thoughts to pass on to others.

As you consider this supreme object of your affection, there are basic questions that could well be considered: Is he/she basically kind? warm? patient? understanding? a good listener? tolerant? willing to compromise in a difficult situation? (If the answer is all in the affirmative, grab that special person quickly before someone else does!)

There are many various serious things to be discussed between a couple before taking the plunge. On the subject of religion, if not the same or similar, discuss how that difference could be handled, especially if children are involved. Considering children, do you have a mutual desire to have them? If so, how many? A discussion regarding financial affairs is also very much in order. And don't forget about making time to meet your future in-laws. There will be many family get-togethers in the years ahead and acceptance and harmony will be very important to you both.

On a personal note, we have an endearing plaque that hangs on our wall. It has two brightly colored turtles happily moving along, side by side. He jauntily wears a blue cap turned backwards and she wears a yellow bonnet tied under her chin. And with this picture are the words:

It doesn't matter where you go,

what you do or how much you have,

it's who you have beside you.

For us, that says it all.

Nancy

*R*eflections On A Happy Marriage

Our 60-plus years of happy marriage are due to:

~ Our recognition of each other's values and interests.

~ Realizing that it is much more enjoyable to share life's content with a spouse.

~ A willingness to praise the other for assistance in solving problems.

~ Never going to bed mad.

~ Being always willing to talk things out.

~ Never forgetting birthdays or anniversaries.

~ A demonstrated willingness to live within financial capabilities, despite the downward fluctuations.

~ Recognizing each other's parents and families as part of our family circle.

~ Being flexible in regard to relocation.

~ Jointly participating in community and political activities.

~ Willingness to ask for and accept spouse's opinions in regard to unexpected situations.

~ Always taking time to display affection for the other.

~ Being sensitive to each other's faults and offering kindly constructive criticisms.

~ Never being too proud to apologize when the other has been offended.

~ Recognizing each other's needs and adjusting behavior accordingly.

~ Acting kindly toward spouse's friends. (CONTINUED ON PAGE 160)

Roland "Bill"

Howard and Iris Kaplan

Married on August 29, 1949
Miami, Florida
His age: 24   Her age: 21

Sun, Sand and Surf: Both Howard's and Iris's families had summer beach cottages in Michigan City, Indiana. Iris and her accompanying college roommate were basking in the sun when they noticed two fine-looking gentlemen nearby — one of whom was Howard. Daring Iris initiated an introduction. Summer love followed.

You marry because you enjoy your husband and want to be with him as much a possible. Love grows with the years as you share experiences and children together.

Marriage is a firm commitment over everything else.

You don't discuss divorce during an argument, and it takes two to argue. You stick to what you're discussing and you don't throw more flame on the fire.

I stayed home and took care of the children and the house. This kept my interest on my marriage rather than "that cute guy at work." I did substitute teaching, medical assisting, Avon, all part-time, at my convenience. My husband knew that he had to "bring home the bacon."

Remember that you come from different homes and you must adjust without insulting your mate's family and habits.

In college I majored in Psychology and I was aware of difficulties women face from failed marriages. I was determined to stay married. I'm glad I did!

Iris

My advice to men who are about to get married is find yourself a gal who is easy to talk to, who has things in common with you such as raising a family **together** and I emphasize together because to make a marriage last, in my opinion, you have to be together on all issues, home, excursions, and bedroom activity. And, the most important ingredient to make a marriage last is letting your wife have the last word in any discussion, at least let her think so.

Howard

Paul and Carol Kurland

Married on June 17, 1951
Mount Carmel, Pennsylvania
His age: 27   Her age: 23

Upon finishing graduate school, Paul and Carol acquired two valuable documents: 1) their diplomas, and 2) a marriage license. During graduate school they were resident interns at a settlement house in Pittsburgh. Paul and Carol formed a close friendship and after earning their degrees, they tied the knot.

Some of the ingredients for a long-lasting marriage would be:

1. The development of mutual respect as well as self-respect.

2. It is important to be independent of one another and also to be interdependent when needed, particularly in old age.

3. Compromise is another major component of a good marriage.

4. Before entering matrimony, it is essential to complete one's educational goals, have a good job with a decent income. Financial stress is not helpful to a good marriage.

5. General agreement on religion, social and cultural values, and on child rearing is necessary.

6. Acceptance of each other's family and the development of mutual friends and a support network is beneficial.

7. Ability to talk about problems, work out mutual solutions and compromises.

8. Important to have one's own interests as well as share in interests of spouse.

Carol

The first thing is to know your partner well. That means, do you have the same values regarding:

1. Your personal relationships together, e.g., division of responsibilities regarding finances, saving and spending money, household chores, parental roles, sexual relationship, social relationships, etc.

2. To what degree do you match well together, to what degree can you compromise?

3. To what degree are you matched educationally, satisfied with each other's work activities, socioeconomic status, religious values, etc.?

To the degree you are well matched, this will facilitate communication and contribute to feelings of intimacy and friendship. Where differences arise, resolve them through discussion. Respect for each other, enjoyment of each other, and willingness to accept that 85% of what you want may be good enough when 100% is not possible.

Paul

Adolph and Fleurette Kurtzman

MARRIED ON FEBRUARY 5, 1950
PHILADELPHIA, PENNSYLVANIA
HIS AGE: 26   HER AGE: 20

Luck of the Draw: A business associate gave Adolph the phone numbers of two young ladies he thought Adolph might like. He dialed Fleurette's number first and asked her for a date. Needless to say, the other girl never received a call.

Words like commitment, compromise and communication come to me.

It helps if you have similar backgrounds and interests and try to grow together. My husband is a tennis player, I'm a bridge player; we learned from each other. These are good social interactions.

Talk about sex and money. Confide in each other.

Society was a help before — divorce was not acceptable, women didn't work and couldn't support themselves.

Projects to do together — house, furniture, children, and vacations.

Sex in the beginning, children in middle, and comfort in the end.

Fleurette

Sex is very important especially for the male partner. We had great sex for the first 40 years. After that, we've coasted.

Learn to share good and bad experiences.

Adolph

Ernest and Esther Levi

MARRIED ON NOVEMBER 27, 1949
CHICAGO, ILLINOIS
HIS AGE: 25   HER AGE: 19

Ernest and a friend picked up two young ladies in a movie theater. The big shots bickered for the older one. (Esther was the youngest.) Who would get her? It was a coin toss! Ernest lost, but soon realized he was the real winner because he became coupled with Esther — for life.

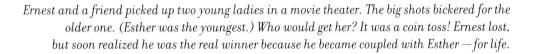

*C*ongratulations — Mazel Tov — We made it. Never thought we would. It's been more than 50 years and let me tell you all — it was hard. But two girls and one son and five grandchildren later, it was all worth it. "God Bless." Young people today have it so easy. One little argument or disagreement and they're off to see a lawyer. They don't know how to talk things out among themselves and then make love (the best part). Of course things are so different today. It's a whole new world and much more difficult, and the only way you learn about marriage is through years of experience — trial and error. I was fortunate in that I didn't have to work, so I was able to be home to raise the children — good and not so good. I think every woman should get the experience of being out in the business world for a short time. But my husband wanted me home. Today that wouldn't go over so good. I'm a little bit smarter through it all, the good and the not so good. It's been a good marriage and we're still at it and still learning. Every day is a different experience. We love each other — we argue and make up. We holler at each other. But most important, we're there for each other.

Esther

I think the first ingredient is to love each other and be able to forgive and forget a lot of things which are not quite the way you would like them to be. To have a long-lasting marriage is more than just living together and having children, although to raise a family is one of the main things in a marriage. I really think there is no such thing as a perfect marriage. There will always be a difference in personality, behavior, manners, tolerance and a lot of other things, but as long as you realize that marriage is a two-way street, I think you can make it last a very long time. As time goes on and you spend more time together, especially after retirement or a sickness, the most important thing in life is to have a companion that really cares for you and tries to be as loving and helpful as humanly possible. As in most cases, I found you cannot depend on family and kids to do everything you require, they have their own problems, so the only one for you is your loving spouse.

Ernest

Alfred and Candida Lopez

Married on May 28, 1952
New York, New York
His age: 17   Her age: 17

She loves me, she loves me not...Alfred and Candida were 12 when they met while living in the same tenement in New York City. Upon reaching dating age, Candida had two suitors — Alfred and Alfred's buddy. Alfred gave her an ultimatum: "You can't have both of us. Make your pick." Alfred was the victor.

When you say "**I do,**" gone are the days of "**Me,**" and "**Us**" begins the rest of your life together. Couples should not just survive or endure their relationship, they must continue to grow and develop. It is also wise to understand that even though you are one in marriage, a well-balanced independent adult could bring untold joy into the marital union. This will help create deep, meaningful loving relationships. Husbands and wives should also become partners and not just cohabiters of the same space. When troubles may come in a marriage, couples should actively seek marriage counseling, self-help marriage books, and attend marriage seminars and workshops to help keep their marriage healthy. Most marriages end for the very same reason — lack of deep, meaningful love. We want to encourage all couples by letting them know we are living in the best of times for having healthy marriages. It is alright to share your pain, ideas, seek help, and be different. We should always seek to make our marriages last, not just endure. To grow together, and not to grow apart. To become partners, and not just two individuals sharing the same space. Above all, the secret to a lasting marriage is "forgive, forgive and forgive some more." The good news is that it never runs out. Take advantage of what we have learned in our golden era of marriage and may God walk with you and bless your union as it has ours.

Candida

God has truly blessed our life, which we have shared for over a half century. In this time, we have known hardship, happiness, and most everything in between. Our journey together began with hope and a promise of a long future together. When we started our new life together, we lived in New York City and it was a new era filled with the potential for a bright future. Along with the promise, however, were the challenges of life for a newlywed couple filled with struggle and strife. However, we never once questioned if it was the right thing to do. We knew that it was right in our hearts. Through our life together, we have been fortunate to receive heaven-sent gifts to include among other things the precious birth of our two daughters and in our later years the special miracle of grandchildren. My closest friend is my mate and we have grown to understand the importance of respect and to appreciate our differences as well as the values, which brought us together in one purpose and in one flesh. A marriage is a living promise, which renews each day for as long as we nurture our relationship.

Alfred

Donald and A. Beryl Lucas

MARRIED ON APRIL 25, 1942
WOODSTOCK ONTARIO, CANADA
HIS AGE: 20 HER AGE: 18

The grand opening of Southside Park in Woodstock, Ontario also marked the grand entrance of Beryl and Donald into each other's lives. Festivities included an outdoor dance, which Beryl attended with a friend. This friend coincidentally went to school with Donald. When Donald was spotted in the crowd, the friend introduced the two.

I met my love just before my 18th birthday. He was 19. We both just seemed to enjoy each other. We continued our friendship, which turned quickly into love followed by marriage. When we came back from our short honeymoon I had scarlet fever. My love took care of me. Two months later I became pregnant, and a few months later my husband went into the Air Force as we were in the middle of World War II. We were so in love. Nothing else mattered. We had little money but lots of love. Every time my honey had a weekend he would hitchhike home. He could be home faster than waiting for a train. We have never been apart more than 10 days even to this date. When our son was eight months old I moved from station to station to all be together. In 1945 Donald got out of the Air Force and we started civilian life together. No one could be happier. In 1947 we had twin girls. We had very limited money but we both worked hard at little things to make life exciting — a nice dinner, his favorite meal, special dessert. Always being honest and caring of each other, always confirming we loved each other. We had two more daughters, in 1949 and 1958. Life was very busy but we always made time for each other and fun.

It is now over 60 years since we met — lots of sickness and ups and downs. We have never had a day that we didn't confirm we love each other.

Our children are all married having families to give us 14 grand-children and 18 great-grandchildren. (CONTINUED ON PAGE 160)

Beryl

I first started to think about "girls" at about age 12 but never gave it much thought until age 19 when I saw this most beautiful blonde girl with this most gorgeous smile in a white shirt and dark skirt. I was smitten! We dated very steady, had a few ups and downs, and I missed her very much when she went home on weekends. I finally popped the question in early 1942 and we married later that year. When we came home from our honeymoon, my bride was sick with scarlet fever.

In the first 16 years of wedded bliss there were many trials and tribu-lations — tears and laughter that make a family grow and share respect for one another. We have a very close bond and are a close-knit family.

I think Beryl and myself have made all decisions together.

A happy life is made up of family, friends, relations, memories and expectations. True love is never having to say you're sorry. Time is endless and only makes you "closer."

Donald

Henry and Corinne Maday

Married on October 1, 1932
Batavia, New York
His age: 21   Her age: 17

Two Wrongs Make a Right: Henry and Corinne were introduced at a swim competition. Afterward, Henry and his buddy gave Corinne and her friend a ride home. Henry got caught speeding and the police confiscated his driver's license. Shortly after, Henry got yet another ticket—for speeding and driving without a license! A dreadful day? No way…because he met Corrine.

What constitutes a platform for a long marriage? This is a rhetorical question. It may have an answer and again no answer for the simple reason there really is no one answer, not unlike "one size fits all." Why? The basic ingredients are well-known to everyone. Each of the individuals in a contemplated marriage will at one time or another be cast on the stormy seas after matrimony. Each will be exposed to the elements. The first prior to marriage is both shall observe a clean and cautious courtship, to eliminate the proverbial "marry in haste, repent in leisure"—an axiom that contrary to many it is not self-evident. Another element and most important is to remember the vows reiterated to one another: in sickness, in health and until death do us part—plus the addendum **Love, Honor, Obey;** each and every one needs to be couched with common sense. In the last of the three…

I do not believe we, Corinne and I, are the only persons, when passing judgement as to marriage whom disregarded the elements I mentioned necessary to have a successful, long married life. We defused the church's admonition that to marry within the concepts of mixed marriages will be the instrument of divorce or annulment.

Corinne, a Lutheran at birth, accepted Catholicism by her own volition.

So how did we accomplish what even we consider eventful? Over 70 years of being together, near poverty during the "'20 Depression," sickness time and again, each administering to the other. The joy of being able to enjoy the blessing of health bestowed upon us by the Lord. The birth of two children who emulated our teachings taught to us by our loving parents.

No, we did not live in the land of all sugar and honey, but we tried at all times to practice, again taught by our parents, not to hurt any one intentionally, since they saw the light of day just as you and I. We often were contrarians in "never go to bed without settling an argument" again —Why? Because the subject matter diminished by morning, not completely, but it made the cause to ask—Why? Then, settlement came easily. I respected her views. I may disagree but she too has reason for her views. And if no solution came, it died a natural death, forget it.

Ah! The last—I have never lost the sense of love for her. We repeat this at Mass in church, and often it just pops out, it comes out as easy as eating her wonderful pie baked for me. Finally we observe the "Golden Rule" and practice it.   AUTHORED BY HENRY

Corinne   Henry

Booth and Corella Malone

Married on March 30, 1946
Washington, D.C.
His age: 28   Her age: 34

Buzz about a very eligible and dapper Air Force officer — Booth — stationed at a nearby military base spread feverishly among the young women of Montgomery, Alabama. Corella and her girlfriends hosted a dinner party for the fine chap. That evening Corella's and Booth's relationship took flight.

*P*riorities for a long, loving marriage are:

1. Be prepared to share everything. You are no longer single.

2. Do things together.

3. Cool off before you start a fight. Give yourself 30 minutes before you discuss your point.

4. Forget the little stuff — nothing is worth a break up.

5. Give your partner a kiss each night and tell him (or her) you love him — even if you are still upset.

6. Start fresh each morning and forgive the past.

7. Enjoy your friends and stay young.

Corella

*O*ur marriage has lasted over 55 years in spite of many prolonged separations due to shifting assignments in my flying career.

Maintain communication during these periods and treat the home-comings as a reunion.

Do things together when you are able.

Maintain a close relationship with your children when you are home.

With your wife maintaining a fixed base for your family, she will have the opportunity to develop a group of friends, so when you are home, do your best to encourage this as a joint effort.

On major decisions such as buying a home and furnishings, work together and try to maintain a common plan to attain your desired goal.

On finances, work together to provide a pleasant and comfortable present, and for a sustainable future.

Our age at marriage was probably beneficial.

Booth

Sidney and Rosalind Mendelson

Married on June 30, 1940
Live Oak, Florida
His age: 23   Her age: 19

"Extraction" of Sidney's wisdom teeth brought about the "attraction" between him and Rosalind. Sidney, bed-ridden from surgery, had company — his cousin and Rosalind's older sister, a friend. Rosalind tagged along. Sidney's pain turned to tingles when he met the "extra" visitor. Upon regaining his health, Sidney ventured out for Rosalind.

Yes, we have been blessed! And, no, it doesn't happen automatically, but on the other hand a loving and caring marriage **can** become automatic. It is so important to love your mate so much that you are willing to compromise even when sometimes you feel you may be right. There is a lot of give and take in a happy marriage — but I don't mean being stepped on or mistreated. Both partners have to give some time — especially if one feels more strongly about something. Respect is very important, so is confidence. It is very necessary to communicate — stay in touch with each other, mentally and physically.

However, I have found that if you **truly** love each other that all the above just happens naturally because you want to make each other happy.

Rosalind

Starting even before marriage I think the couple needs to analyze as carefully as they can those areas that may be troublemakers after the ceremony, such as religion, possible career conflicts, thoughts about having a family, whether both are tidy (or not), and so on. Things like these, and many others could be major problems after the euphoria of the wedding is over.

Ours has been a very good marriage, not that we didn't have spats from time to time, but we never went to bed without kissing each other goodnight and saying "I love you." I recommend this to all newlyweds. Incidentally, the disagreements steadily declined over the years and we learned to give and take more and more.

Basically it's a good idea to determine who feels the strongest about a dispute (if you can) and let the mate with the strongest feelings about the subject prevail. It's not necessary to "win" every disagreement. Also, you need to take into account the pressure your spouse may be under at times and be more tolerant than usual.

Children can really put a strain on a marriage if the parents don't cooperate to head off possible conflicts between each other. To avoid the potential conflicts, we usually delayed an answer to the child until we could talk it over privately with each other, unless it's a matter we knew from experience what the answer would be.

Basically you need to be completely dedicated to the marriage and have taken your vows seriously. Your mindset should be to do those things that will make your spouse happiest and you will find that your spouse will, in almost all cases, do the same.

Sidney

Charles and Dolores Moench

MARRIED ON SEPTEMBER 3, 1949
POINT PLEASANT, NEW JERSEY
HIS AGE: 23   HER AGE: ~

The warmth and security of family and friends was palpable following World War II as evidenced by many joyous gatherings. For example, in Point Pleasant Beach, New Jersey, Dolores's and Charles's families attended a Mass and reception celebrating a friend's ordination — where the two met. Their later union — one of complementary natures — created yet another joyous event.

My Recipe For A Happy Marriage

Two people (1 male and 1 female) who can Love, Accept, **Respect,** and Communicate. Have a great deal of Patience, Kindness, Self-Control, **Commitment,** Faith, Hope, Truth, and a large dose of a **Sense of Humor.**

Use all of the above Daily.

Then, daily throw away

Jealousy, arrogance, and selfishness

And go for the "gold."

Dolores

Marriage is hard work! But the rewards have been immeasurable. Like what happens when an immovable object meets an irresistible force.

We were married at a young age from today's point of view. Most of our friends were or were about to be married. Money was scarce and advice was plentiful. Neither was important. Our pleasures were simple; the world was open to us. All we had to do was work for what we wanted.

The secret, if there is a secret, is that we both came from families and homes where we were made to feel like special people. We have tried to carry that with us in the way we treat each other and our children. As a matter of course, it carries over to our relationship with everyone we come in contact with.

That doesn't sound difficult, or, where is the work? And this is the hard part: Each of us is an individual with our strengths and weaknesses, our highs and lows, our needs and desires, our wants. But life is like a maelstrom, a tornado, ready to rip us out of the ground and toss us in all directions. We have successes and failures. There is complete joy and utter disappointments, even sorrow.

We, as a married couple, experience all of these daily to some degree. Having another to share them with, always mindful of their individuality, is a major reward,

The key — you have to work at a marriage to make it work — every day, every hour.

Charles

Marshall and Mary Morgan

Married on April 7, 1951
Iuka, Mississippi
His age: 18   Her age: 17

Bologna, salami, ham…While slicing and dicing, a romantic relationship was cooking behind the meat counter at H.G. Hill grocery store. Marshall was a meat cutter and Mary was a meat wrapper. Their "job satisfaction" was off the scales.

*M*arriage is a life-long thing and you go into it with that on your mind — to love your mate forever. Never go to bed mad at each other. Always make up. Never buy large items without you both being willing to do so. I wish I had known about saving for the future when we married.

*A*fter serving in the military for 12 years, I went to college, became a minister and have been preaching over 40 years. I wish I had known and understood the Bible more and better. In it and through the practice thereof I have learned what love and sacrifice are. The Bible truly teaches one how to love God, to respect and love his wife. When one "does right he feels right." One must learn to respect himself before he can respect others. It has caused me to never want to do or say anything that hurts my wife, causes her to feel bad about herself or to disrespect her in any way. For she is truly a great lady and that makes it easy to love and respect her. Had I known more about trust in the beginning, it would have prevented a great deal of jealousy on my part. I also wish I had known how to save for the future at an earlier age.

Laurence and Florence Myers

MARRIED ON OCTOBER 22, 1933
PROVIDENCE, RHODE ISLAND
HIS AGE: 28   HER AGE: 23

Meet the Parents: When introduced by mutual friends, Laurence was enraptured. Florence, however, thought she still wanted to play the field. She invited Laurence to dinner to meet her mother and father. Her parents voted unanimously in favor of their guest, and Florence made her final decision.

Since I was 23 and my husband 28, I believe we were ready for marriage. I would advise a couple planning their marriage to be loving, kind and truthful to each other. Also, a couple who prays together stays together. That has been our philosophy all through our 70 years of marriage. Yes, we had our differences of opinions, and also misunderstandings. But with love and understanding each other, we always made things right before we retired at night.

There are some things I would do differently if I could call back the years. All couples have to make adjustments the first year of marriage. It takes time to get really acquainted with your new husband.

As I look back when I was young, I had several boyfriends. I know I made the right choice when I married the best man, Laurence.

Florence

When we met, Edna was a trim, beautiful young lady 22 years of age. I was a slender 6'2", 27 year-old, a college graduate. We have found the ingredient for a long and happy marriage is this: both have a love for Jesus. If she is telling a fact of something in the past and you do not exactly agree with her, clamp up. Sometime later in a soft, conversational tone of voice talk it out. Got a good book which you both enjoy, then spend the evening sitting close on the love seat reading to each other.

Be happy, tell her so. These practices have brought us 70 years of happiness.

Laurence

Marty and Ruth Nash

Marrried on February 23, 1943
Miami, Florida
His age: 22   Her age: 21

At a USO dance, Marty was playing a game of checkers when his concentration was distracted by a pretty gal, Ruth, standing across the way. Marty made smart moves on the checkerboard, but his best move that night was introducing himself to Ruth.

*I*ngredients for a long-lasting and happy, loving marriage are: Consideration to spouse, compromise, caring, forgiving, paying attention, listening, admiring accomplishments, pride, interest, respect, support, enjoying and developing common interests and hobbies, overlooking small annoyances, not letting differences grow out of proportion before settling the issue, and putting your spouse always first in your thoughts.

A large dose of the above ingredients should add up to a wonderful, great marriage of 50 years or more.

Ruth

*S*taying married is a "part-time" job…The rest of the time is spent enjoying your partner's company.

For a man to stay married to one woman for over 50 years, there are several requirements. Your partner must be respected, honored, caressed, loved, protected, comforted and supported.

Couples that "enjoy together…stay together." It's so important that you both enjoy the same things in life…for example…travel, the theater, dining or the great outdoors. Whatever is the choice, it needs to be enjoyed by both.

With the fast pace of life today, young people miss the excitement of a real honeymoon when marriage really begins. The old song title comes to mind…"Love and Marriage…can't have one without the other."

Marty

Juan and Maria Ocasio

Married on July 30, 1949
San Juan, Puerto Rico
His age: 21   Her age: 23

Riding the bus drove them to lust. Juan and Maria resided in the same neighborhood in San Juan, Puerto Rico. Their jobs, too, were located in the same proximity. As a result, they commuted on the same bus to and from work. Their final destination, however, was the wedding aisle.

*I*n my opinion I think for a long-lasting and loving marriage, both need to love each other very much. With this love comes understanding, respect, trust, and perseverance. Sharing the good and bad situations together. Also forgiveness plays an important role in the marriage.

I would say to a couple about to get married: know your man, his family, his beliefs, but most of all ask God for guidance. I did, and I did get a response — a good and everlasting one.

Maria

*O*ur marriage was based on love and respect, also trust in each other. Be sure that your fiancé feels the same way you feel for her. Study very well what your situation and hers is. Always count on "Our Lord" for guidance and strength, and you will grow together with the woman you love.

Juan

Milton and Gertrude Pincus

Married on March 15, 1943
New York, New York
His age: 25   Her age: 22

Theories and formulas. Who cared? Studies were secondary to the sparks that flew between Milton and Gertrude in their Economics class at City College of New York.

There are many ups and downs in marriage but our love and respect for each other has carried us through.

Have patience; bend when you have to. I'm still learning not to criticize too much.

My mate tries very hard to please me. He's always there when I need him. He is my best friend. He has not always been receptive to my wishes but eventually we will compromise.

Life is beautiful, try to enjoy it. Be happy that you have each other. Accept the trials and tribulations; look at the bright side.

We've had our share of differences many times, mainly about trivial things. It is always wonderful making up, hang in there.

I don't know if anything I had known before marriage would have made a difference. Life is an every day experience and it would be wonderful to be able to cope with each new situation.

Be supportive of your mate. Be generous with praise and love. Respect his family as well as yours. Forget about trying to change each other, that is an impossible task. Try to adjust. Good luck and fortitude is needed.

Gertrude

It has always been my belief that a marriage must go through a period of adjustment. The length of time depends on the individuals involved. This may take years, but I see it as a necessary element for a successful marriage. Unfortunately, there are many who are not willing to put the time and effort into this important phase of their lives.

On the other hand, there are those who stay in unhappy marriages for many years for the sake of the children. This I believe is wrong, since it is very likely that the offspring are aware of the troubled marriage and can be adversely affected. This union should be terminated before it is too late.

Then there are those couples who claim they never argue. This indicates that one is always giving in to the other in order to keep peace in the family. This does not settle anything. Any disagreements should be resolved satisfying both parties.

My advice to newly married couples is:

Give the marriage time to gel, don't rush things.

Respect your spouse.

Never go to bed mad.

I wish I had known more about the female psyche, sensitivities and thinking before I married. That knowledge might have made things easier at the beginning.

Milton

Kenneth and Louise Precht

Married on August 12, 1945
Baltimore, Maryland
His age: 20   Her age: 20

In the third grade, as they were walking to elementary school, Kenneth's carefully aimed snowball hit Louise. Louise turned to see who the crankster was and Kenneth proudly confessed his mischief. Twelve years and countless snowball battles later they became permanent allies.

I married the most wonderful boy in the world. The good Lord above brought him home safely to me and I promised to be his wife for the rest of my life. The best advice I can give a young person today is to be sure this is what you really want for the rest of your life, that is a very long while. To be faithful, loving and kind. Try to understand him or her. Do not try to change him or her to meet your requirements, because if he or she really loves you he or she will be agreeable. Always talk things over and never go to bed without saying "I love you" and really mean it. If one of you gets sick, be there for each other. You can't have things always your way, you have to give in sometimes. When one of you gets angry with the other, there is always a way to work it out. Just remember sex is never the only way to love each other. You need to have deep feelings for each other and to be able to forgive each other and forget.

Louise

I would advise a young person about to marry to "feel mature enough." What I mean by that — know what you want in the future, a good wife, children, a home, a decent job? Don't approach married life for reasons of sex, easy living, or because you're fond of the other person. You have to feel love deep down in your heart; so deep; **so** deep you know it! Your wife should be your **best friend**.

After the honeymoon, a good marriage doesn't just happen — you have to work at it every day. Make it work! Both of you do as many things as possible "together."

Keep God and prayer in your lives.

Share your feelings about money matters, your jobs, your likes, dislikes, everything. "**Communicate**." If you have arguments, don't say things that hurt each other. Never go to bed at night angry, and always, the last thing both should say is "I love you."

Be willing to give up your single independence or **don't** take that big step. Be **proud** to be married. (It's not easy!)

Kenneth

Fabian and Inés Roman

MARRIED ON NOVEMBER 11, 1951
FAJARDO, PUERTO RICO
HIS AGE: 23   HER AGE: 21

*T*he first step for a happy and long marriage is true love. Communication is a must. Bad feelings must never be kept in for a long time as they will turn into resentment toward the other person. We must always forgive each other, especially before going to bed. Prayer is very important. Feeling connected to God gives us the strength to forgive, and as I mentioned, when there is true love it is easy to forgive. Respect is also very important.

I am happy because my husband loves me and is very patient with me. When I am sad he makes me feel happy.

In order to have a good marriage, respect is very important as is being responsible in the home. Greet your husband with love when he comes home from work. Don't burden him with complaints of the day's events.

For the younger generation, my advice is to get to know each other very well before getting married. Get to know, respect and accept each other's families. And most importantly, marry for love and not convenience.

Inés

*O*ur relationship developed through friendship ties between our respective families. However, the most important ingredient that brought us together was the love born from the knowledge and respect of each other's differences. I believe that you cannot love a person unless you ignore your differences and accept your "partner" for a long-lasting partnership. It is fine to call it marriage but I believe it is better to name it "Partnership." We joined to develop a life relationship that would entail discovering and resolving our daily challenges.

Some of the most important ingredients to maintain and preserve a long-lasting "Partnership" are faith in God, prayer, loyalty, fidelity, honesty, resolution, forgiveness, fun (not taking yourselves too seriously and thus denying yourselves time to have fun with each other and life experiences), togetherness (we have tried to always be together in everything we do), and backing each other up on whatever we decide to do. But, above all of this, the utmost goal in our relationship is to be able to increase our love for each other **"Daily."**

Fabian

Robert and Beatrice Saffer

MARRIED ON OCTOBER 31, 1948
BUFFALO, NEW YORK
HIS AGE: 24   HER AGE: 20

Ooooooooouch! Beatrice's sorority sister at New York's State Teachers College invited Robert to a picnic. At the outing, he noticed a cute young lady — Beatrice. To meet her, Robert accidentally poked Beatrice in the tush with a fork! Fortunately, she has a good sense of humor. Soon after, they switched to hugs and kisses.

After more than 50 years of marriage, it's hard to say what goes into a lasting marriage. When you marry, realize the person you married is an individual and will most likely not change their personality or character; learn to accept. Stand by his side in all endeavors, and don't expect the impossible.

Raising children together is very important; do not feel your way is the best.

Above all, like your husband, not just love him.

Beatrice

We have been married as of 10-31-2003 (Halloween) for 55 years. That adds up to 20,088 days allowing for leap years. Of those 20,088 days, 20,087 days have all been good. That's not too bad a record, considering how many things I do that are wrong. My wife ignores most of my bad traits (which I have many of). She also has a few, which I try to ignore.

We have had our ups and downs, financially as well as health, etc. But we have overcome all of these because of our love for each other. We have had our share of fights (not physically, of course) but always **tried** to go to bed at night and forget the past day. (It's always fun to make up.) We still fight, but we still love each other and I would still do it all over with the same girl. **Overlook a lot of things.**

Sigmund and Roberta Safier

Married on March 16, 1947
New York, New York
His age: 29   Her age: 24

"The family that prays together stays together" but for Sigmund and Roberta, it was prayer that joined them. During World War II, Sigmund was stationed in Lincoln, Nebraska. At the same time, Roberta was a student at the University of Nebraska. Roberta's father, who met Sigmund when he spoke at their synagogue, later introduced them.

I believe that the first and foremost ingredient for a happy marriage (besides love itself, which should be assumed) is mutual respect. There will inevitably be disagreements, but it is important not to say things that you will be sorry for later — and to never go to bed still angry with each other.

When the time comes for raising children, it is important to have more or less the same philosophy about raising them, and when you differ (and you will at times) to discuss those differences away from your children.

As far as advice for newlyweds is concerned, I would hope that they would enter into marriage aware that there will be difficulties at times, and that one has to work at marriage to make it work. I would hope that they would not enter into marriage without a certain degree of maturity, and with something more than a strong sexual attraction.

Roberta

*W*hen we were married, there was no such thing as pre-marital counseling. You had to depend on your **instincts, love and "good" judgement.**

In courtship, we discussed our aspirations and goals. We loved one another and felt very comfortable together. Unlike the world of today, divorce was not in our vocabulary. Our rabbi's blessing, the shattering of the glass, and Mazel Tov was all we needed.

Then the fun began. Little by little we realized that we were different in many ways and our approach varied. I learned her ideas and she learned mine. Being comfortable and respect for each other is most important. Talking and listening are paramount.

Neither of us has ever been jealous. I'm always concerned that Roberta has her own identity and pursues her interests like mah jongg, needlepoint, bridge, cooking and her friends.

Basic advice that I would give to newlyweds would be as follows: Finances should be simple; **set budget** and **establish a joint account**. Also never go to **bed angry**, resolve differences and don't carry grudges.

With the advent of children, we agreed on unified decisions — never pitting one against the other. A firm policy for both of us — No spanking, there are other ways.

Sigmund

Alvin and Rose Savage

MARRIED ON AUGUST 23, 1942
WINSTON SALEM, NORTH CAROLINA
HIS AGE: 26   HER AGE: 21

When Rose first set eyes upon Alvin, he was wearing a misproportioned, white-linen suit featuring high-water slacks and just-below-the-elbow coat sleeves. But, she was so taken by "the best-looking man I ever saw" that she didn't notice his apparel faux pas. This incident occurred when Alvin was visiting his cousin, and a date had been prearranged with Rose.

In the early years, I think just being in love was enough. As we matured and raised a family, my husband devoted most of his time to his profession and I allowed him to do his thing. I was solely the child raiser and homemaker. Of course in those days I had full-time help, so it was much easier than today.

I think respecting each other's interests is important and giving each other permission **willingly** to pursue their hobbies — Alvin's was fishing, golf, raising orchids, making jewelry, many meetings doing community and professional jobs. I do admit the only way I know I let him down was not becoming a good bridge player!

To this day I try to put his needs first **willingly** — it's never a chore to do things for a wonderful husband. It's important to appreciate what life has given me in him, as my partner, my friend, who is always there for me. He also has a great personality, and I still laugh at those jokes I've heard 100 times!

Now that we're in our 80's, we always care for each other physically, and I try to keep up his morale when he is discouraged. I am a **very** lucky person!

Rose

As I think back, what where my thoughts before marriage? Before I was married, I had no concept of the ingredients that made up a marriage much less than what constituted a marriage good or bad…We were two people who felt comfortable with each other and loved to be together all the time.

The only advice I received was from my mother who said "be sure to allow your wife freedom, particularly in regard to how she spends her allowance you may give her."

Those were the days when the wife did not work and stayed at home. However, during the years, many things began to develop. Those problems were solved with mutual understanding. I was given the freedom to do what I thought was best for the family, and my wife had the same freedom. We accepted and encouraged what each desired.

The most important single factor was the knowledge that we were faithful to each other and never knowingly did anything to make the other unhappy.

The one problem we could not solve was how we raised our children. That was because of different backgrounds.

The advice I would give to newly married couples today would be:

1. Listen and respect the opinion of your mate.
2. Be faithful and honest with her.
3. Make your love visible and honest.

If I had known all of these things before, life would have been very dull and boring!! You must live it first to be able to enjoy your life in later years.

Clarence and Margaret Schwartz

Married on January 12, 1943
Elizabeth, New Jersey
His age: 25   Her age: 24

Absence Makes the Heart Grow Fonder: Throughout high school, Clarence and Margaret were familiar with but indifferent toward each other. No flirting. Not even a wink. The tide shifted when Margaret moved out of town. They began dating!

*I*t takes more than love, respect and patience to make a good marriage.

Ours started during the war with my husband in the army. When I joined him I had never been on my own. We didn't have much money in those days, and with kids coming early I didn't know about budgeting or putting money aside for both necessities and vacations.

Because I was an anxious mother, wanting our kids to have the best, i.e., dancing lessons, parties (to which my husband agreed), financial problems were always in the background that put a strain on our relationship. I feel it's important for couples to know how to spend and save their money.

Also, it was difficult for me to be at home with young children and realize that my husband was in an office with young women with the same business interests as he did and for me not to feel insecure and jealous.

Fortunately we had the dedication to overcome these challenges and have made it through more than 60 years. As I said at the start, it takes love, respect and patience to make a go of it.

Margaret

A loving and lasting marriage takes a lot of doing. First off, you have to choose the right partner. Is this someone you want to spend the rest of your life with? Do you have some of the same interests? Are you compatible intellectually? Are your backgrounds similar? You really don't get to know someone until you've lived with him or her. In our day, this was a lot tougher to find out than it is now. Couples didn't live together before marriage. Maybe today is better. If you've made a mistake, it's easier to fix than divorce, which often involves children and can damage their lives as well as your own.

Things can get very hairy in a marriage, especially at the start. That being said, the key word in a marriage relationship has got to be "compromise" — you win some, I win some — but always there has to be a certain amount of giving by both partners on the important issues, regardless of how strongly one or the other may feel about bringing up kids, how and where to spend money, where to live, what color to paint the walls, and thousands of other family matters. At the same time, both opinions have a right to be aired and seriously considered before decisions are made together.

Further, any loving husband should understand that bringing up kids, housework, cooking and doing what wives do, while necessary, is drudgery. (CONTINUED ON PAGE 160)

Clarence

John and Lucy Setaro

MARRIED ON MAY 3, 1941
CHARLEROI, PENNSYLVANIA
HIS AGE: 24   HER AGE: 25

Love at first sight. It vanished. Years passed. It reappeared. The first time John and Lucy met, they were at a beach in Pennsylvania. They gazed, smiled and exchanged a few fleeting words. Poof! Lucy was gone. Five years drifted by. One Sunday night, their lives again crossed at a local dance. John spotted Lucy, and they got their second chance.

ove is the main ingredient. Love brings trust and understanding and a willingness to share and share alike. It helps hurdle the obstacles of life. Respect is also necessary.

I would tell those who are planning their marriage that they have that commitment to each other to make a good marriage. Really enjoy each other's company. Be a friend and be courteous, respectful and helpful. Be "one of the family" and treat them as if your own. Respect each other's opinions. Children and finances have to be discussed. Enjoy some activities together. Also, have some interests of your own.

Lucy

rust and foremost, be sure you love her before you marry. Get to know her, her family, her friends, her likes and dislikes. Be understanding and considerate.

Advice, as above, but also read up on subjects such as marriage and all it entails, re: compatibility, rearing of children, finance, household management, and handling of family crises.

Above all, do not "control" your wife, children and household. Share and share alike and be considerate.

My marriage, initially, revealed my ignorance of most matters pertaining to being a good husband. Being of the same background, both of us with loving and caring parents, was a plus!

John

Francis and Marian Shuman

MARRIED ON JULY 27, 1942
FRANKLINVILLE, NEW YORK
HIS AGE: 29   HER AGE: 19

Low on toilet paper, Marian's mother drove Marian to the grocery store to run in and replenish. Francis was the store manager. When Marian saw the distinguished-looking fellow behind the cash register counter she dashed out of the store, too embarrassed to get the toilet paper. So Marian's mother traipsed in to buy it. Francis carried the bags to her car and consequently, he met Marian. Shortly after, Francis called Marian for a date.

It takes awhile for two people to learn to get along in a marriage — it doesn't happen overnight. We all have shortcomings that we may not even be aware of until our mate points them out to us. Go into the marriage determined to make it successful and not with the idea that "If it doesn't work I will just get out."

This is not a game — these are very serious vows that you are about to make before God and are not to be taken lightly.

I believe that a sense of humor is very important — it helps to be able to laugh at the silly mistakes that happen to you.

Talking to couples about to marry I would urge them to be careful of family background — you may not think that you will be involved with the rest of the family but you will be.

Make sure that you have some common interests — if he loves to hunt, fish and camp and you like to party — it will be hard to mix these lifestyles.

Just because you grow old and wrinkled doesn't mean that you can't have fun — keep your love alive and the companionship in your later years will be worth all your struggles.

Have a church home and take your children with you.

I wish I had known before entering marriage that my husband was not an affectionate person. He is very good to me and has seen to it that I have a nice home and all the material things that I needed. So many times though I would have been glad to trade some of these things for a few extra hugs and kisses.

We've been married over 50 years and we're still friendly most of the time. Ha!

Marian

Find a girl with good parents and a good family life. Her parents were the best.

Francis

Marvin and Beatrice Simkins

MARRIED ON MARCH 3, 1946
PHILIDELPHIA, PENNSYLVANIA
HIS AGE: 27   HER AGE: 25

After a long week of college studies, Beatrice went to a Friday night get-together at a friend's home. Marvin dropped by with a buddy, who knew Beatrice's friend. Marvin noticed a bright-eyed, smiling young lady — Beatrice — sitting at the baby grand piano in the living room. An introduction was made and together they achieved perfect harmony.

*I*t is my contention that marriage is an evolving process. It takes work, cooperation, patience and fortitude to make it succeed.

My generation was programmed for marriage, children and happily-ever-after in that order, without any sort of preparation or foreknowledge, but plenty of unrealistic expectations, fostered by movies and romance novels.

It's been almost 60 years, some good, some not so good, but we finally got it right. Family tragedy and health problems have brought us together, and have enabled us to find a deeper, more lasting love.

I would recommend what I call the 3 C's for marrying couples:

1. Consideration
2. Communication
3. Compromise

All three are important to **both** partners and should be observed and followed. The rewards will be something to look forward to.

Beatrice

*F*or me, "getting it right" has been the essential but difficult process in fostering a successful marriage.

In spite of all the homilies which claim to "insure" a good marriage, the solution must be addressed on a marriage-by-marriage basis.

How the couple copes with all-too-frequent challenges posed by life situations determines the strength or weakness of the union.

In my particular instance, I have had difficulty curbing my self-absorbed agenda and am still working on that aspect.

Without accommodation, flexibility, empathy, cooperation, consideration, love, friendship, respect and a sense of humor, it would be most difficult to build a lasting relationship.

My wife and I, who are now in our ninth decade, have substantially reached a point in our marriage where we are comfortable, and have a relationship that is enjoyable and enduring.

John and Catherine Slodysko

MARRIED ON JUNE 29, 1946
COAL TOWNSHIP, PENNSYLVANIA
HIS AGE: 27   HER AGE: 23

John and Catherine were regulars at the local skating rink, a popular retreat for neighborhood kids and teens. Around and around the rink they circled, and as they did, their relationship grew and grew.

*L*ove, Respect, and Communication are the most important ingredients in a marriage. Everyone has disagreements at some time, but if you talk about them, everything will work out. It is not hard to do. When children come, try to be a stay-home mom if possible. It worked fine for us. You do without a lot, but it is worth it. Neither of us smoked or drank liquor or beer so we didn't do much partying. We usually went everywhere together and with the children. We also attended church together until the children went out on their own. Having enough family time is very **important**. Never go to bed angry. This is important.

If someone is planning on getting married, the best advice I could give is make sure he **respects and loves you**. Don't worry about having a new car, furniture, etc. These items should be second. Enjoy life and thank God for all your blessings.

Catherine

I believe and know that you should show respect to every girl you meet. I always was polite to Catherine, and everyone else I met.

As Catherine and I dated, I found out how beautiful and lovely a person she is, and how she respected her own mother and that there was a very good love between them.

I thank God for leading me to her. In our almost 60 years of marriage, we have always been together — to church, to a movie, to parks, and to see good shows ("clean ones").

We always help each other out. When either of us got sick, we would pray to God to help us get well. I am a very lucky man to have a wife. I have faith and trust in her.

This is why my marriage is so happy and clean. We never "hide or hold" anything from each other. God really blessed us.

My wife gave me three beautiful children who are all married. So far we have five grandchildren. We are very happy for what God has given us.

I came from a family of 12. Yes, I had seven brothers and four sisters. My family was poor, but we all were healthy and strong in our faith.

I would never change anything in my life. Remember? What you do to others, they will do for you. My mother's famous words were: "Remember in your life, you make your own bed, now lay in it."

John

Golden and Mary Alice Smith

MARRIED ON DECEMBER 23, 1951
JACKSONVILLE, FLORIDA
HIS AGE: 30 HER AGE: 25

Rather than order "take out," "take in" was a weekly tradition during the Smith's courtship. Golden's Sunday special delivery of a juicy hamburger and yummy vanilla ice-cream to Mary Alice not only quenched her appetite but won her heart while they were students at Bethune-Cookman College.

Basis to achieving a long-lasting and loving marriage is Faith — Faith in God, Faith in one's self and Faith in the mate. Undergirding the Faith is Love — Love that is profound and sincere. Qualities and characteristics required to build and sustain a strong marriage are: prayer, faith, love, patience, understanding, kindness, unselfishness, the ability to compromise and a willingness to forgive and forget.

Our marriage has lasted over 50 years because as a wife I strive to adhere to the qualities and characteristics just mentioned and I try to treat my husband the way I want to be treated. This means not being too judgmental or critical but supportive and willing to listen. My husband and I study the scriptures and pray together. This, I believe, has and is sustaining us in a long-lasting and loving marriage.

My advice to a couple about to be married is take time to help make the marriage work and keep a positive attitude.

Prayer is the key.

Mary Alice

My experience for achieving a long-lasting marriage has been a deep abiding Faith in God. My love for my wife goes back to our college years. (It was love at first sight.)

That love has grown and grows because we both worked hard to be mindful of each other's feelings and desires. I have helped to sustain this strong marriage by adhering to First Corinthians 13:4-7 verses:

"Love is kind and patient never jealous, boastful, proud, or rude. Love isn't selfish or quick tempered. It doesn't keep a record of wrongs that others do, and love rejoices in the truth, but not in evil. Love is always supportive, loyal, hopeful and trusting."

My advice to a couple about to be married is to Trust in God, as well as each other. Rely on God's Word to help in times of trouble. Have faith in God and pray.

Golden

137

James and Mildred Stark

Married on April 6, 1941
Pittsburgh, Pennsylvania
His age: 23   Her age: 23

The Gift of Gab: At the University of Pittsburgh, James's fraternity brother was stuck on the phone with his chatterbox date for an upcoming dance. As James was passing by the exhausted lad grabbed him. He told his date, "Here. Talk to James" and tossed him the phone. She asked James if he had a date for the dance. "No," he replied. She promised to fix him up and, finally, hung up. Mildred was the blind date.

When young people ask me how I could stay married over 60 years (!) I tell them 60 years and 10 divorces!

Advice to cope with the 10 divorces:

1. Surprise! **He** isn't perfect and **he** doesn't think **I** am either! Develop a sense of humor.

2. Unite to cope with in-laws.

3. Problems over his friends and mine. Make new friends.

4. Children: enjoy, enjoy, enjoy and cope, cope, cope with the challenges of raising children.

5. Share chores. Only two boys in my husband's family and they had to do girl's work for their mother and I got the results of their training.

6. When the husband is "down," be sympathetic and encouraging. Don't, don't blame!

7. Together cope with financial solutions.

8. Be there! In sickness and in health.

9. Aging. Giving each other only **true** compliments. Well, maybe once in awhile, a sweet untruth!

10. No solution, no person is perfect, not even **me**! Cope! Face the challenges.

Marriage is a shared adventure of learning. To know and understand each other brings rewards: true lover, true friend.

Mildred

First: I always wanted to have a family and a home.

Second: Meet girls at group parties, and double-date with other couples — like ourselves in personality and ambitions.

Third: The girl I was seeking is sincere and a good listener. Our conversations revealed our feelings about our life together. We felt comfortable with each other physically and mentally. When sitting, dancing, walking to classes, movies, and to the park, we felt we could accept each other's aims for a good life. We accepted the financial positions for a teacher in a city school system.

Fourth: Get to know her family to see if I fit in with them and they accept me.

Fifth: After being married and establishing a few years of family living, we became more open and honest about our plans and desires. We worked all our years at finding a solution to our differences with compromises.

My wife is still the same sweet, understanding girl I married. I couldn't have done it with out her!

What do I wish I had known before matrimony? Since I was inexperienced in sex, I wish I had known more about how to please.

P.S. Enjoy life with each other. We made changes to make our home comfortable — refinished a 10-piece dining-room set and rearranged the room structure. We camped across the USA, pursued extensive international travel, and we had 10 summer school National Science Foundation scholarships. We enjoyed all and they helped in binding us together. Aging together intensified the love and need for each other.

James

Maynard and Mary Stone

Married on June 22, 1935
Ferndale, Pennsylvania
His age: 24   Her age: 23

Vampires and witches and ghosts and goblins haunted Maynard's and Mary's ghoulish meeting at a Halloween party. Dressed in costumes, they removed their masks and revealed their true selves. From that spooky night arose a lifetime of love.

The first four years that we were married both of us had full-time jobs. When I became pregnant, we seriously discussed my keeping my teaching job. I needed help so I asked Maynard to help me with some of the household tasks. We really enjoyed doing the dishes together and still continue doing them together. When a new problem came up, we would discuss the situation thoroughly and try to do something that was fair or helpful to both of us.

Waiting four years before having children gave us an opportunity to get to know each other's habits and ways. This was a big help to us.

We lived in the area where I taught, and we raised our two girls there. Of course we had babysitters who stayed with the girls and took good care of them. I continued to teach for 35 years in the same school district.

In the nearly 70 years that we have been married we have had adjustments to make, but it can be accomplished if both of you desire it. We feel blessed that we could be together this many years.

Teaching was a good profession because the summer time could be used beneficially for traveling and family trips.

Mary

As Mary and I started dating we talked many things over about matrimony. After four years of dating we married. Our eldest child was born after we were married four years, and our second child was born seven years later. We lived close to the children's grandparents, which was convenient because they often kept both children when we were busy. The children loved their grandparents and were eager to visit them.

We always felt the reason we got married was because we enjoyed each other's company and wanted to be together. That is the main reason we stayed together so long.

Maynard

Leonard and Marion Suskin

Married on January 16, 1949
Bronx, New York
His age: 25   Her age: 22

"Got a match?" was Marion's pick-up line to introduce herself to the cute guy — Leonard — at a synagogue dance. Leonard responded "No," but then asked her for a dance. In fact, Marion did get her match!

We were very fortunate that we both came together and wanted to have a loving home. My husband came from a divorced home with a stepfather he did not love. I came from a broken home since my mother died when I was three years old. I lived with many different people. We shared this need for a close relationship. We had our differences but learned to be forgiving. Our sex life was also very good. We made friends with people that were well mated. We made it important not to have friends that were incompatible since I believe if you go out with people who complain it could cause you to do so.

Marion

Make a concentrated effort to meet each other half way and a serious effort to avoid arguments.

Leonard

Ross and Helen Tipton

Married on September 25, 1937
Oxford, Indiana
His age: 27 Her age: 22

Ross's date for the high school prom contracted appendicitis. That emergency ignited another one: Who was going to be Ross's date? An acquaintance of his, who also was Helen's roommate, came to the rescue by fixing up Ross and Helen.

In our generation, divorce was not an option. I think we all realize that being kind to our mates made life more pleasant for both. The Depression was still on and a 5¢ chocolate ice-cream cone was a real treat.

We both came from solid family backgrounds and have many interests in common — our children, music, fishing, bridge, cooking, travel, a spirit of adventure, and now our computer — but each also has separate interests. Ross enjoys sports of all kinds on TV (now in his 90's, he still plays golf) and I read several books a week and enjoy oil painting. Fortunately we have been able to fix most physical problems that have arisen.

As for advice: Get to know each other before marriage. We were married four months after we met and have had many surprises for each other. Ross is a Leo and I am a Sagittarius and many sparks have flown. We were lucky and were able to work out our differences but it would have been easier if we'd known what to expect.

~ Don't marry hoping to change your mate — it is not likely to happen.

~ Be sure you choose someone you not only love but also will like after the first bloom has worn off.

~ And don't overlook the physical side of marriage. Making up after a spat has smoothed many rough roads.

We have had a wonderful life together and marrying each other is the luckiest and smartest thing we ever did!

Helen

When dating, try to imagine living with this person for the rest of your life. Try to think of the mental qualities as well as the physical. Once married, stay together as a couple. If you travel, take your wife with you every time possible — that way there is less chance to stray. Become aware of your wife's likes and dislikes and try to do things that you feel will please her. When children arrive, try to do your part as a parent. Try to keep the same standards for discipline as your wife. Things have changed so much in the last few years that a father must take more responsibility since most wives must work to help support the family.

To young people getting married, there is more to marriage than sex. Sex is a very small part of marriage. You will spend many hours with your wife so plan things to do together that you enjoy. Understand that there will be days that things will not go as you planned. Don't blame your wife. Never be physical or abuse your wife, she is in no way able to return this kind of action. If you feel that you are losing your temper, find some way to get away until you can think and regain your composure and cool off.

Before I was married, I had no idea what marriage would be like. What would it be like to have the same person around all the time? How and when would I find time to do the things I wanted to do? The sex was important but what would we do with the rest of our time together? How hard would it be to provide for two rather than one? What would we like for us in the future? Will our marriage succeed?

Ross

Richard and Mary Rose Tobin

Married on November 30, 1946
Louisville, Kentucky
His age: 29 Her age: 26

Here comes the Bride. Not Mary Rose — yet. The wedding of Richard's cousin and Mary Rose's best friend provided the occasion for Richard and Mary Rose to meet. A little more than one year later they took their own stroll down the wedding aisle.

Thoughts on how to have a loving and lasting relationship: strong faith; love that deepens as you grow older together. Common interests and communication. Have differences of opinions, but listen to the other side. Try not to go to bed and to sleep with hurt feelings on both sides. It has happened, but rarely. Deep faith, deep love and respect for each other. Always, but always, keep a sense of humor.

Mary Rose

Herewith are a few of the essential ingredients, which I believe helped Mary Rose and me enjoy a successful marriage:

1. **Commitment** — Marriage is a sacred contract made in the presence of God and is a commitment between a husband and wife agreed upon for life. You mutually pledge to accept the positives and negatives that go with the union. Consequently, the longer two people are together, the more ways each learns to cope with the ups and downs of marriage in order to preserve the special union "until death do us part."

2. **Faith** — Is the glue that keeps the marriage union whole: Because Mary Rose and I, as Roman Catholics, share and practice the same religious beliefs, that is a most favorable ingredient of our union. If it were not for our faith and prayers to God, I do not know how we would have survived the rough spots.

3. **Communication** — The right hand has to know what the left hand is doing and thinking at all times. Each partner is entitled to know the aspirations, fears, emotional concerns about job employment, financial matters, children's problems, etc. When we do have a serious disagreement, we pledge not to go to bed that night without first reaching some sort of agreement, sealed by a kiss and expressing our genuine love for each other.   (CONTINUED ON PAGE 160)

Richard

Rubin and Sonia Weiner

MARRIED ON FEBRUARY 19, 1950
PHILADELPHIA, PENNSYLVANIA
HIS AGE: 22   HER AGE: 22

The Weiner's story began when the Pilgrims sailed to Plymouth Rock in 1620 and Thanksgiving was declared. For without this holiday, the two may never have met. Rubin returned home from college for Thanksgiving. During his break, a blind date arranged by a mutual friend set Rubin and Sonia on their own lifelong voyage.

There had to be an initial attraction. For me it was this handsome, smart, kind, sexy man. We had fun together and I loved him. Our more than 50 years have had continuous ups and downs, but we always clung together with support, trust, and devotion. Having similar backgrounds helped to understand each other's values and goals. Whatever happens, stick together, remain loyal, and encourage the other to attain his/her goals. At certain stages of life we mature and grow differently, and we need to understand what is happening. Listen, listen, listen to what your spouse is saying, and sometimes we realize we're in the wrong. Try to change your behavior and your spouse will automatically change his without even realizing it and you'll grow closer. Work at it all the time, never let up, then when your children leave, you'll realize it was worth it, and the joy of sharing your senior years together is the best. Do for each other, be kind to each other, and try to be understanding. It's never easy, but it's all worth it. Your later years can be the best ever, it's so comfortable, so lovely to just be together, to do for each other and enjoy the good times. Life is short and loaded with adversities — work them through together and reap the benefits. The tough times can be so bad, you want to shuck it all and you're at a loss about what to do. Don't give up, don't go back to mom and dad, work it out yourselves, the rewards are endless. Talk, talk, talk — read together, learn together, love together, travel together, work hard together and play together. (CONTINUED ON PAGE 160)

Initially, we fell in love much the same way that other couples do — we were first attracted to each other for our physical and mental attributes, plus similar cultural backgrounds. Then, over the course of time in going together, we realized that we wanted to stay together and get married. We had no children for five years, and enjoyed going to concerts and shows together, and had a wonderful circle of friends.

I worked and went to school part-time until I received my degree, and Sonny helped and supported me throughout. Then, when we had children, I tried to help in any way I could. When Sonny decided to go back to work, I tried to help and support her in that, so we worked together to take care of our home and children. When we moved, I appreciated the effort she made to establish us as a family in a new environment, becoming friendly with neighbors and co-workers.

We joined a new synagogue and became active in its programs, including teaching in religious school. She helped me learn to celebrate holidays with new-found friends. We learned together how to go camping, and took our kids on some camping trips. I was happy to take the kids to activities or on a weekend camping trip, so Sonny could have time for herself. When I had activities, such as playing tennis, that she couldn't participate in, she never objected, and vice versa.

Even though we may have had arguments, we always tried to work them out so as to continue without dislocation. (CONTINUED ON PAGE 160)

149

Beryl and Marilyn Weinstein

Married on March 12, 1950
Jacksonville, Florida
His age: 23   Her age: 21

Down by the boardwalk…Beryl and his cousin were lodging at Jacksonville Beach, Florida. The cousin was friendly with Marilyn and knew she, too, was visiting the beach. He told Beryl, "There's a real cute gal from Lake City staying here." With that promising description, Beryl's interest was peaked and the cousin arranged their rendezvous at the boardwalk.

A marriage cannot always be perfect. It takes time and patience. Respect each other's feelings and share responsibilities. There should be a lot of communication — say what is on your mind — be open.

After more than 50 years of marriage, you start thinking alike, your personalities almost become one. Sharing the same hobbies and interests can make a marriage strong but the couple should have separate interests as well.

A strong marriage will bond a strong family. Children bring everything together. You set the example.

Love is the strongest ingredient and don't forget to say you love each other.

Marilyn

One of the major ingredients to a successful marriage is to realize that you will experience ups and downs along the way; that your "life partner" and you may **not always** agree, but each of you must respect the other's opinion. You don't have to always be right — there can be another viewpoint. Don't make an issue about small matters. Maybe give in (if necessary) on some points so that you can be more firm on major issues. You must give each other space to do the things you are interested in, although you should try to develop mutual interests that you both enjoy. Family and friends are very important — especially family.

Beryl

Joseph and Ruth Esther Wittenstein

Married on August 11, 1938
Orlando, Florida
His age: 24   Her age: 22

It's a Small World: Joseph and Ruth Esther were childhood friends, growing up in what was then the small town of Orlando, Florida. School, synagogue, social events and more — the two frequently associated. As a result, they shared innumerable memorable experiences long before officially starting their lives together.

*F*irst — a brief summary:

1. Live within your means.

2. Have some fun.

3. Make a good circle of friends.

4. Participate in your children's activities.

5. Be demonstratively affectionate.

A lasting marriage is something we both work on every day. First and foremost is love and real respect.

Joe has given much community service, and has immersed himself in our children's activities.

He tries to do things that include me and pleasure me — trips, etc.

I had a good example of a very loving marriage — my parents.

We have been faithful to our marriage vows.

Courtesy is important and so is honesty.

Ruth Esther

*T*here is no such thing as pre-marital training. Children learn from experiences by observing their own parents. Each of us was raised in wholesome households. Both sets of parents were good citizens. Each family had the respect of their peers, performed public service, and participated in school, religious and community activities.

This served as role models for me and my spouse as the way to guide our own lifestyles.

Joseph

Sam and Kitty Wynn

Married on August 3, 1940
New York, New York
His age: 22   Her age: 18

"A bag of bones" wasn't exactly a compliment, but Sam meant it only in jest when he met Kitty. He and the slim teenager were at a touch football game at a local park. Sam was playing and Kitty was spectating. A mutual friend introduced them...Touchdown!

*H*aving met my husband (to be) when I was only 14 years old I now wonder how I had the audacity to think I could choose a lifetime mate at such a tender age. However, we did have four years to become friends before he finished college and we married.

Each of us has always been concerned with the other's happiness and well being. We have deferred to one another ("No, you take the last piece of candy!") in matters large and small and almost always come to a happy agreement.

I guess we've been a good example for our three happily married daughters who have over the years referred to us as "Ozzie & Harriet" (an unlikely ideal couple of parents in an early T.V. series called the "Nelsons.")

My advice to young people getting ready for marriage would be: Know each other well, become friends first and have an abiding respect for love, loyalty, trust and each other.

Kitty

*W*e met and fell in love when I was 18 and Kitty was 14. (I thought she was almost 16 – until she confessed several years later, when I was finally hooked!) She waited four years, while I finished college, so we learned about love and life together.

The pressures of school, work and my mother's biased attempts to break us up (due to our different religions and backgrounds) almost succeeded, but our deep and abiding love prevailed!

Shortly after Pearl Harbor, I was called into service as an infantry officer, which lasted over four years, with periods of separation and togetherness. The birth of our first two daughters in 1943 and 1945 will give you some idea of how glad we were to see each other!

We often disagree, but now we call them "debates" and never hold grudges!

We try to be reassuring to each other and understand the other's point of view. We have found that our mutual love and respect has grown every year of our marriage.

The last thing we say to each other nightly is "Goodnight…I love you."

My recommendation to a couple about to be married is to be sure you really know and love each other and are making a lifetime commitment!

Sam

Annette Alpert

The gemstones, the perks, the real plusses will be the grandchildren and the great-grandchildren who come along and prove the beauty and the rewards of the union.

Only after the many years of hard work and committed effort do we realize that we have succeeded, only to be one day separated by death of one of the partners.

At this time (in my opinion), the proof of the depth of the love and commitment comes with the realization by the survivor that someone must be a part of his/her life; not to replace the former partner, but rather to fill the need of completion.

David Alpert

In our opinion, it is most critical for the survival of a marriage that children are a part of it.

9. Our financial situation has always been sound. There were times when we had to struggle with money problems, certainly in the early years of marriage, as well as some later periods. Neither of us was born with a "silver spoon"; therefore, what we have was acquired with hard work.

Winnifred Bartholomew

Oh, yes a sense of humor is very important. When you have a problem and you're really upset and your spouse can crack a joke and you can laugh, you've got the problem licked. My husband is very stubborn, and that I would change if I could but everything can't be perfect. He plays the organ too loud but he always remembers to put the toilet seat down!

A happy marriage means you have been forgiven a lot and you have forgiven a lot. I really think the key word to a long marriage is **forgiveness.**

Raymond Bartholomew

I relate to all who will listen that a marriage that doesn't get gooder will get stale and fail. Anything worth having is worth working for, but because of the great reward in a successful marriage the word "work" has to take a back seat to pleasure.

Truth and honesty must be kept at a maximum to attain the peace and joy that comes from two people becoming as one. It is easy for me to write on this subject because I could never have been happier. My wife has made it so easy to relate to our marriage that I would love to shout it from the roof. The word "unity" puts the whole consensus of a great marriage together. The three S's for a sermon outline is now called for: Stand up, Speak up, Shut up.

Jane Benjamin

In this final stage of life, more than 60 years together, we are finding time for memories and reflections.

Our bodies are a constant reminder that we are now octogenarians. Luckily there are some fringe benefits. Our five senses are in tact. Our senses of humor are still with us – that helps!

Slowing down has given us the opportunity to observe and enjoy a blooming flower, a sun shining day, a child's happy face. At last things are in a proper, better perspective. Best of all we still have and love each other.

Helen Bronson

Sometimes in my husband's deep mental struggles concerning problems on his job, he always knew that I was always by his side to give emotional and spiritual support.

Trust is most essential to a successful marriage. I always felt that my husband was honest and reliable. I had no reasons to doubt his integrity and good intentions for our marriage and our children. He never questioned my faithfulness nor my love for him; neither have I doubted his love for me.

Both of us resolved prior to our wedding to take our marriage vows seriously. We felt that divorce was not an alternative to solving any problems that often develop in marriages. Rather, we resolved that we would remain together "until death do we part."

Our home has been a place of joy, fun, learning, character formation and family worship. Our family worship was reinforced, strengthened and inspired by our attendance and participation at public worship and gatherings.

Oswald Bronson

There is always the danger of responding to one's own mistaken perceptions of what is being said rather than what the marriage partner is really seeking to convey. Further, it is also healthy to allow the other to share her/his true feelings without becoming defensive. This requires "listening" not only with our heads, but also "listening" with our "hearts."

Fourthly, we gradually learned early the importance of taking time off in a pleasant surrounding — to be alone with each other. Sometimes a dinner, or later, the blessing of an affordable cruise, or a night in a hotel, or simply a breakfast at our favorite restaurant would suffice. These moments alone enabled us to nurture our relationship, put misunderstandings in proper perspective and reinforce our romantic feelings for one another.

Finally, we resolved to engage in family worship with our children and with each other. Family worship served to remind us that it takes more than human love to keep a marriage wholesome; it requires a Divine Process and Presence beyond the human.

Lillian Capko

Although Mike is in his 80's, he has not retired. When he leaves for work, he kisses me goodbye. When he comes home at lunch and at the end of his work day, he kisses me hello. When we go to bed, we hug and kiss each other good night. Some of our kids have picked up on this habit, too. Hugs and kisses have kept our marriage together.

The last reason our marriage has been long lasting goes back to the very beginning of our marriage. We took our vows for better and worse. Good came with the bad. We focused on the good, not the bad. There was nothing we couldn't handle if we handled it together. We also made a promise to never go to bed angry with each other. We had to work it out and go to bed happy.

From our wedding until now, we have had a great marriage. Mike and I met young (he was 17, I was 16) and we will die old together. We understand each other and think alike. We thank God for our children and our years together. We have a wonderful life together and our family will continue because of our children and our love for each other.

Michael Capko

Jean, our first born came while I was in Europe. She was nine months old before we got to be together as a family again. It might have been longer but lucky for us I made a difference in the European Theater because the Germans gave up 10 months after I got there. At least I told Lill that!

Our marriage has produced 5 children, 20 grandchildren, and 3 great-grandchildren.

I was blessed with a terrific and understanding wife. She works hard for our family. Even at 80-plus years old she is depended on by our family and contributes to help make life easier for anyone who needs help. It makes me feel good when she comes to me to give me a hug and says, "You know, I love you." We have made it this many years because we started out slowly. We mixed a sense of humor in with doing things together and loving each other and our family.

Sidney Charschan

We have had disagreements but would not try to battle it out by imposing our will on each other. We would not talk or kiss each other good night (a regular ritual) until we cooled off. But then the sex was great. It still is! We do care for each other and not pick at faults — which we both have, and don't say things that will be regretted. We share the duties in the house. I take care of the outside and pay the bills, while she takes care of the inside and balances the books. Please God, at least another 10 good years together.

Arthur Cohen

I do believe I thought about many of these issues before marriage. But the test is in the doing. Thinking, verbalizing about issues may all abort before the doing and just continue to stew. One tough matter is balancing out public and private, i.e., when to share (the good, the bad, whatever) and when to contain, not engage.

Marriage or more precisely family is the institution in society meant to provide intimacy, support and respite free from the severities and pressures emanating elsewhere. If valued, one need be prepared to work hard at making it succeed. Whether it does or not, be assured it is not written in the stars. It doesn't just fall into place neatly, nicely. You must work at it, at times work hard. You give and you grow.

Joan Farrar

Ron became a college professor; I became many things — teacher, real estate broker and lawyer.

As to bringing up our children, we were in complete agreement. We would let them decide on a religion when they were old enough to make the determination for themselves; and they did. One became a Jew, one a Christian, and one undetermined. We never ever contradicted each other's decisions once made. For instance, if I would tell one child that he could not do something, the child learned not to go to Ron and ask the same question. Because Ron would always say: "Have you asked mom? What did she say? Then why are you asking me?" We always backed each other up that way. Our decisions on important things were always made after discussion. When the children were young, Ron and I made the decisions. When the children were older, they were included in the discussions and their opinions were listened to.

I think we became better friends when we retired and were spending proportionately more time together. We have had fewer distractions and have been able to concentrate more on ourselves as a couple. We still have disagreements, but know that we can work them out with patience and compromise.

Ron Farrar

She is bright and accomplished and far more proficient than I am in everyday things but she accepts all the many things that she has done with disparagement. In any case, regardless of this fault which I wish she didn't have, I love her dearly — far more than at the beginning of our marriage because now I realize all of the things that I caused her to tolerate. In other words, we get along because I have been able to change my behavior and attitudes over the years — although she still can become irritated with me (and sometimes I with her). I have also learned that the words "please" and "thank you" are invaluable. When I think of all the people I could have been entangled with, I find myself almost grateful to the point of tears that I ended up with the girl I did.

Lillie Fleming

It is important to live each day to the utmost of its possibilities. Let no day pass without finding some richness in the moments that were given you by the grace of God. Total happiness does not consist of the abundance of things possessed, but rather upon the value placed on them. Be happy with what you have.

Leon Fradkin

In every marriage there are times when argument and anger threaten to bring on a degree of dissatisfaction that threatens the marriage. It can be about children, money, sex and plain boredom. The main reason for our success in surviving is our sense of humor. We seem, in most cases, to see humor in our disagreements which we use to lighten or melt the anger. In the early years Louise would assuage my ego by letting me be the winner in an argument. Now, in the later years of our marriage it is my turn to back off. I ask myself, "Is it rational to stay angry and stressed out? To deny myself the pleasure of a happy wife to satisfy my ego?" I decided early on I had two choices: to stew with my anger or give Louise a kiss and make up. In most cases I choose the kiss. Now I have added a 10-second hug with the kiss. It is amazing how 10 seconds of her warm body melts away my anger.

In the early marriage years the need to pay our bills was the major problem that we had to focus on. It left little time for any other problems. Then came raising children. That alone creates the glue for a marriage. As the years pass by, the rocks in the marriage bed can be sex or boredom. Fortunately we are reasonably content with sex. Our interests have taken different roads as the years have passed. We have developed many individual interests that keep us occupied and happy. We still need each other. We still enjoy the warmth of each other's company. I am still proud to introduce Louise as my wife. I still find enormous pleasure in her smile and her touch. In short, I am content.

Gilda Gittleman

Meanness, unkindness and vindictiveness have no place in marriage.

Be a loving parent to your children. Discuss disagreements about them privately. Children should not have to take sides.

Allow family fun time frequently.

Discuss money matters and plan together for spending and saving. Compromise.

A sense of humor is a definite asset. Save the anger for important issues. Learn what is important and what is trivia. So your wife threw out the bean salad by mistake. Handle the trivia. Discuss important issues. Anger can learn to be controlled.

Louis Goldberg

It is imperative that both husband and wife **really like** each other in addition to loving each other. **It's really not the same thing**. It's possible to love somebody, but not like that person for some "not-so-obvious" reasons (i.e., various habits that annoy you). This makes communication and compatibility essential!

Eleanor Gorecki

I think one of the best compliments my husband has paid me was "You are not only my sweetheart but also my best friend." I feel the same way.

We have had a lot of problems and tough times over the years and still have our moments, when we get on each other's nerves, but I am still happiest when we are together.

One thing that I remember was that the children (and the dog) and I always ran to the door to meet him when he returned from work. He told me that no matter how tough the day had been, he knew he would get a hug, a big smile and a good dinner.

We are blessed with many long-time friends and have had lots of interests together and alone. Outside interests make a more interesting life for all.

Charles Hough

She also treated her three sisters to a resort vacation. We've been to Mexico together and separately. I used to go to Penn State football games — sometimes with my wife, but on other occasions by myself or with other (male) friends.

Roland "Bill" Jones

~ Being punctual when meeting deadlines or appointments.

~ Being concerned about spouse's happiness.

~ Taking proper steps to end spouse's unhappiness.

~ Always trying to include spouse in your activities and explain why when it sometimes cannot happen.

~ Always graciously accept spouse's apologies.

~ Share each other's interests as much as possible.

~ Never pick out one child as the favorite over the others; try to treat all children equally.

~ Always trying to maintain a united front in addressing solutions to problems with the children.

~ Participating and rejoicing in children's achievements and successes.

~ Offering kindly constructive criticism when reviewing a child's failure.

~ Assisting children in planning their futures.

~ Yield gracefully to your spouse's strengths.

In short, treat your spouse and children like you would hope to be treated — always remembering that it is the little things in life that matter.

Marriage is not all "peaches 'n cream"; but if you both work at it, it can be a wonderful experience! Face difficulties together — two heads are generally better than one when it comes to solving problems.

A. Beryl Lucas

We have lots of family get-togethers. We all get together once a month for a barbecue or picnic, whatever they plan. Love is caring and being together and doing for each other. Always share your love and your caring. Never forget to say you're sorry! Our children are just as caring and loving and our grandchildren are too. They all love being together and doing things with Mom and Dad.

"Loving is caring."

Clarence Schwartz

Lending a hand is considerate and doesn't make a husband less macho if he changes a diaper, washes a dish, mops a floor or takes out the garbage. A loving wife should show the same consideration for her husband where she can.

It helps to have enough money to finance a marriage; lack of it can threaten its stability and is the cause of lots of bickering. Both should handle it responsibly and preserve it for a comfortable retirement.

As I said, marriage takes a lot of doing. An occasional cocktail helps, too, from time to time.

Richard Tobin

4. **Shared Interests** — Couples who share mutual interests and enjoy doing the same things together usually are successful in marriage. We enjoy travel; reading; bridge; dancing; dining out; operas; theatre; walking; and probably most of all watching our two daughters growing up through 16 years of formal education; maturing to adulthood; getting married and finally presenting us with grandchildren, so as to start the cycle all over again.

Sonia Weiner

There's value in separation at times also. It expands our worlds to meet others and to pursue our own hobbies and individual interests. Then, when we're together, there are new things to talk about and to learn from each other. Work at your marriage, you'll never be sorry. The key words are love, respect, and sharing.

Rubin Weiner

Over the years, not only did we love each other, but we liked each other and respected each other as individuals, as partners, and as grandparents. And a kiss and a hug and a squeeze occasionally does wonders.

Joy • Devotion • Caring • Hugs & Kisses • Fun • Harmony • Communication • Patience • Com
ompanionship • Laughter • Hope • Passion • Contentment • Romance • Sharing • Desire •
Togetherness • Love • Understanding • Joy • Devotion • Caring • Hugs & Kisses • Fun • Harmo
Trust • Honesty • Bliss • Kindness • Companionship • Laughter • Hope • Passion • Contentm
Thoughtful • Happiness • Forgiving • Togetherness • Love • Understanding • Joy • Devotion •
Inspiration • Empathy • Faith • Giving • Trust • Honesty • Bliss • Kindness • Companionship
Soulmate • Enthusiasm • Supportive • Thoughtful • Happiness • Forgiving • Togetherness • Lo
Patience • Compassion • Dedication • Inspiration • Empathy • Faith • Giving • Trust • Honesty
Desire • Humor • Commitment • Soulmate • Enthusiasm • Supportive • Thoughtful • Happiness
Harmony • Communication • Patience • Compassion • Dedication • Inspiration • Empathy •
ontentment • Romance • Sharing • Desire • Humor • Commitment • Soulmate • Enthusiasm • Su
Caring • Hugs & Kisses • Fun • Harmony • Communication • Patience • Compassion • Dedicati
Laughter • Hope • Passion • Contentment • Romance • Sharing • Desire • Humor • Commitmen
Understanding • Joy • Devotion • Caring • Hugs & Kisses • Fun • Harmony • Communication
Bliss • Kindness • Companionship • Laughter • Hope • Passion • Contentment • Romance • Shar
Forgiving • Togetherness • Love • Understanding • Joy • Devotion • Caring • Hugs & Kisses •
Giving • Trust • Honesty • Bliss • Kindness • Companionship • Laughter • Hope • Passion • Conte
Thoughtful • Happiness • Forgiving • Togetherness • Love • Understanding • Joy • Devotion •
Inspiration • Empathy • Faith • Giving • Trust • Honesty • Bliss • Kindness • Companionship
Soulmate • Enthusiasm • Supportive • Thoughtful • Happiness • Forgiving • Togetherness • Lo
Patience • Compassion • Dedication • Inspiration • Empathy • Faith • Giving • Trust • Honesty
Desire • Humor • Commitment • Soulmate • Enthusiasm • Supportive • Thoughtful • Happiness